Palmistry
The Art of Reading Hands

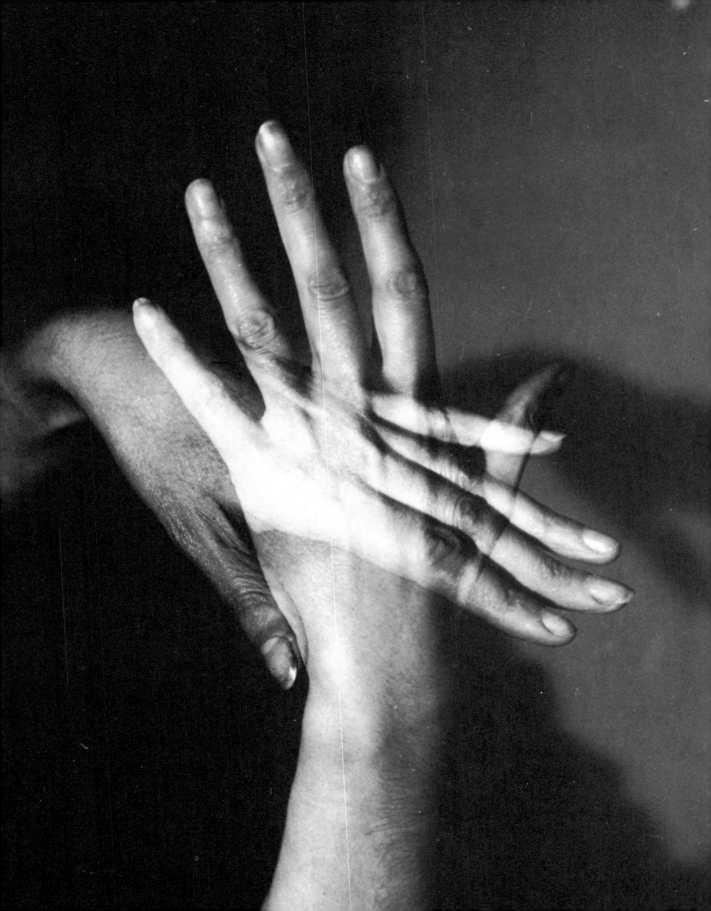

Palmistry
The Art of Reading Hands

by Jean-Michel Morgan
Translated by David Macrae

Ariane Books

Contents

1 – A very ancient branch of learning . . 5
2 – The physionomy of the hand 13
3 – The study of the hand in classical chiromancy 23
4 – The principal lines of the hand 39
5 – Other lines and signs 67
Note – Psycho-physiology of the hand . . .103

Albin-Guillot 12, 14, 15a, 19, 66 — Alinari/Giraudon 8, 98b — Almasy 16c, 20, 29a, 31b, 58a, 60b, 75, 105 — Arch. 8a, 8b, 9a, 10, 11b, 22a, 40, 61, 83a, 89a — Babout/Rapho 32 — Bulloz 54, 99b — Boyer/Viollet 38 — Doisneau/Rapho 73 — Farkas/Fotogram 4, 5, 16a, 23 — Frederic/Rapho 6 — Frieman 25, 26, 28, 29b, 34, 36, 44, 70/71, 100b, 31 — Giraudon 18a, 55, 58b, 91, 92, 98a, 99a — Gontas/Fotogram 74 — Harlingue 57a, 88 — Limot/Rapho 15c — Mayer/Magnum 46 — Maltête/Rapho 102 — N.D. 57b, 83b — Pfaltzer/Viollet 37, 101a, 101b — Scala 17 — Schneiders/Rapho 93 — Stanfield/Rapho 35 — Warnek/Vloo 45 — Weber/Fotogram 107 — Viollet 2, 9b, 11a, 14b, 16b, 21, 22b, 27a, 27b, 42a, 52, 59a, 59b, 60a, 62, 80, 82, 89b, 90, 102.

Printer, Industria Gráfica, S.A.
Tuset, 19 Barcelona San Vicente dels Horts 1975
Depósito Legal B. 23575-1975
Printed in Spain

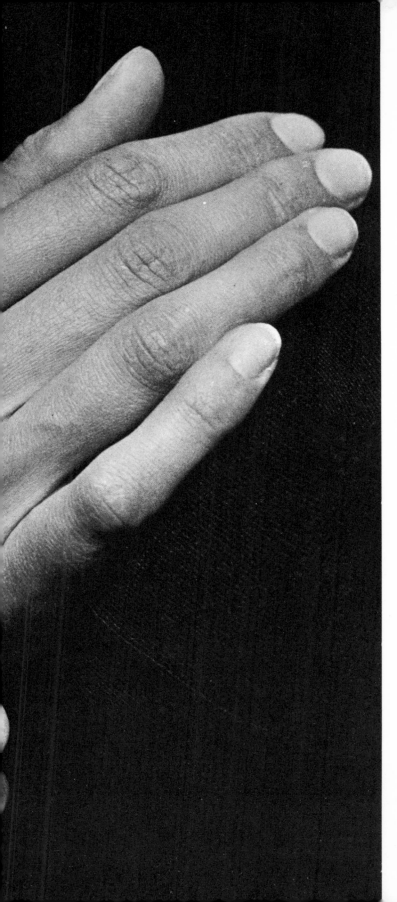

1. A very ancient branch of learning.

The hand has been studied in two different ways by what has come to be known as the "psychic sciences": the first of these, *chirognomony*, deals with the appearance, or physiognomy of the hand; while the second, *chiromancy* or *palmistry*, involves foretelling the future from an examination of the lines of the hand.

These two sciences are really one, in actual fact. The first of them, *chirognomony*, does not concern itself with the future at all; it merely analyses present phenomena, with no prophetic intent, its sole purpose being to study and classify the human character on the basis of an examination of the hand. Chiromancy, however, is wholly devoted to divination; it aspires to seize upon the mysterious patterns of the future, and reveal the broad sequence of events in men's future lives.

Most of the vast body of literature which has been written on the hand consists of re-hashed versions of the major writers on the subject, together with the contributions of lesser figures.

Anaxagoras, the prominent naturalist of the Greek school, was among those writers of ancient times who mentioned the value of chirognomic inspection as a way of determining indi-

vidual character. His theory of *homoemeries* accords perfectly with his cosmological conception of man. Democritus, Artemidoris, Chalchindus were only a few of the writers of antiquity who engaged in chirognomic research; more recent writers on the subject include Cardinal d'Ailly, Savanarola, Père Niquet, etc., although their contributions, on the whole, consist of merely personal observations. The *Astrological Mirror of the XVII century* deserves to be read; it is a curious book, with a rather naive-sounding text which should not deter the reader from studying the great abundance of detailed documentation which it contains; amongst other things, it has a most unusual, and highly rewarding, system for the classification of hands.

The history of chiromancy is much better known.

Until the first half of the 19th century, most particularly, little use was made of the phenomena of chirognomony, consolidated in a single science: chiromancy. The ancients were not merely familiar with the principles of this science, which, in any case, are easily within the reach of the most ordinary intelligence; they had gone further, and had begun to use them in a most creative way. Traces of chiromancy are to be found in the Kabbalah. Chiromancy was a highly esteemed branch of learning in India, and also among the Chaldaeans, the Egyptians and the Hebrews of ancient times.

As a historical aside, we should here mention the curious, and still unresolved problem of the origins of chiromancy; did it come into being independently of, or was it merely an immediate application of astrological science? No serious work has been written on the subject—nothing more than an assortment of vague opinions.

Throughout the Middle Ages, and even in modern times, chiromantic treatises have at-

tached great importance to the transposition of astral horoscopes to chiromantic divination.

Besides the terminology of chiromancy itself, serious students of our subject habitually devote a great deal of attention to virtually the whole of astrology, and the cabalistic signs, which abound in treatises of Kabbalah and astrology.

It would certainly be interesting to study this evolution. We shall simply mention it here, as a whole book could easily be written about it, in the light of the abundant documentation available, and the historical value of the codified human beliefs involved.

Some authors, particularly the Danish psychologist Alfred Lehmann, have maintained that chiromancy had an independent origin; there is much to be said in favor of such a thesis.

However, it is important to remember that most treatises on chiromancy were, by the admission of their authors, based on much earlier Arabic or Greek works, few of which have survived.

Greek thinkers such as Aristotle, Anaxagoras, Plato, Ptolemy and others saw great significance in the lines of the hand and regarded them as a valuable adjunct to fortune-telling. The Stoics and the Peripatetics used to engage in discourses on chiromancy. The Pythagoreans habitually judged the mind and character of people through the lines on their hands and face. Aristotle is known to have sent to Alexander the Great, his distinguished pupil, a book on chiromancy, written in gilt lettering, which had been found on an altar to Hermes; he accompanied it with the most flattering recommendation. This book, originally written in Arabic, was translated into Latin.

Anaxagoras held that man's superiority over the other animals was due to his ability to use his hands, and to the strength of his upper ex-

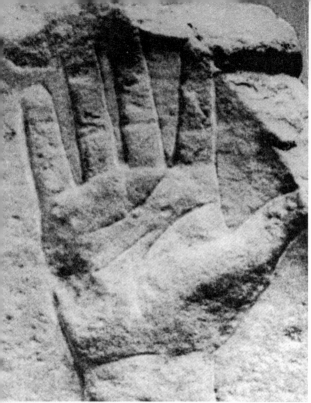

Left: on a sculpture from Delos, a hand, and, already, its lines are accurately reproduced.
– Title page of a book on chiromancy, 1531.
Right: title page of an English work, 1651, and a German engraving, 1466: "the lines of the hand as a mirror of health". Note the religious figures.

tremities. In his *Treatise on the Parts of Animals*, Aristotle devotes one superbly written page to a criticism of this belief. In the 18th century, Helvetius and various other thinkers revived interest in Anaxagoras' thinking. Here we give the gist of his argument.

Nature has given man hands and arms instead of the fore limbs and feet of the other animals. Man is the only animal which stands upright, because his nature is essentially divine. The privilege of this divine branch of the animal kingdom is that it can think.

"Now it is the opinion of Anaxagoras that the possession of these hands is the cause of man being, of all animals, the most intelligent. But it is more rational to suppose that his endowment with hands is the consequence rather than the cause of his superior intelligence. For the hands are instruments or organs, and the invariable plan of nature in distributing the organs is to give each to such animal as can make use of it; nature acting in this matter as any prudent man would do. For it is a better plan to take a person who is already a flute-player than to take one who possesses a flute and teach him the art of flute-playing. For nature adds that which is less to that which is greater and more important and not that which is more valuable and greater to that which is less. Seeing then that such is the better course, and seeing also that, of what is possible, nature invariably brings about the best, we must conclude that man does not owe his superior intelligence to his hands, but his hands to his superior intelligence. For the most intelligent of animals is the one who puts the most organs to use; and the hand is not to be looked on as one organ but as many; for it is, as it were, an instrument for further instruments. This instrument, therefore,—the hand—of all instruments the most variously serviceable, has

The Book of
ALMESTRY
And
HYSIOGNOMY.

been given by nature to man, the animal of all animals the most capable of acquiring the most varied handicrafts."

Later in the same work, Aristotle says:

"For the hand is talon, hoof, and horn, at will. So too it is spear, and sword, and whatsoever other weapon or instrument you please; for all these can it be from its power of grasping and holding them all. In harmony with this varied office is the form which nature has contrived for it. For it is slit into several divisions, and these are capable of divergence. Such capacity of divergence does not prevent their again converging so as to form a single compact body, whereas had the hand been an undivided mass, divergence would have been impossible. The divisions also may be used singly or two together and in various combinations. The joints, moreover, of the fingers are well constructed for prehension and for pressure. One of these, also, and this not long like the rest, but short and thick, is placed laterally. For it were it not so placed all prehension would be as impossible as were there no hand at all. For the pressure of this digit is applied from below upwards, while the rest act from above downwards; an arrangement which is essential if the grasp is to be firm and hold like a tight clamp. As for the shortness of this digit, the object is to increase its strength, so that it may be able, though but one, to counter-balance its more numerous opponents. Moreover, were it long, it would be of no use. This is the explanation of its being sometimes called the great digit, in spite of its small size; for without it all the rest would be practically useless." (Aristotle—*On the parts of animals*).

The arrangement of the nails on human hands was also designed, in the same way, by the Nature that Aristotle unceasingly admires. The

9

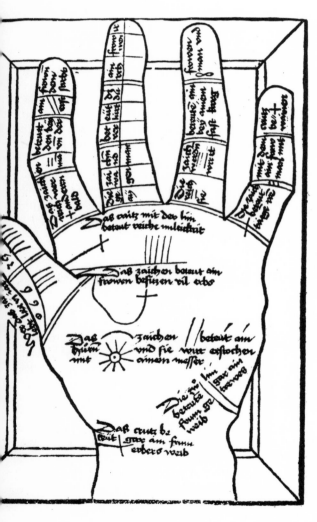

other animals have nails because they need to use them; man, however, has nails which serve to defend and protect the tips of his fingers. The nature of the purpose for which the human body has been designed also causes the arms to bend in a manner different from the arm movements of the animals, this difference being related to the technique of eating used by humans. In Aristotle's own words:

"For their fore limbs are not analogous to the arms and hands of man". Later in the same book, he goes on to say: "It is this hand-like office of the anterior limbs which explains why in some of the polydactylous quadrupeds, such as wolves, lions, dogs, and leopards, there are actually five digits on each forefoot, though there are only four on each hind one. For the fifth digit of the foot corresponds to the fifth digit of the hand, and, like it, is called the big one. It is true that in the smaller polydactylous quadrupeds the hind feet also have each five toes. But this is because these animals are creepers; and the increased number of nails serves to give them a tighter grip, and so enables them to creep up steep places with greater facility, or even to run head downwards."

Chiromancy was certainly in fashion in Rome in Juvenal's day, to judge by the references the poet makes to it in his sixth Satire.

Virgil and Plautus both made it plain in their writings that they were familiar with chiromancy and took a real interest in it. Amongst the Romans in general, and more particularly in the city of Rome, chiromancy, in spite of the Skeptics, ranked as one of the methods of divination studied by the College of Augurs.

Artemidoris, a contemporary of Antonin the Pious, wrote a book in defense of chiromancy. It has been lost; but, judging by the same writer's fascinating *Interpretation of Dreams,* it must

Illustration from "Die Kunst Ciromancia

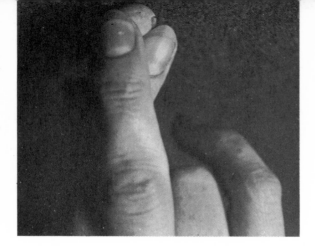

have been a book of some considerable merit.

Lucius Sylla, Caesar and Augustus were reportedly skilled chiromantists. Josephus, the Jewish historian, wrote that Caesar was so accomplished that it was "impossible for any man whose palm he had seen to deceive him in any way; in fact, one day, an individual came to him claiming to be Alexander son of Herod, and Caesar promptly recognized that he was an impostor as he had no mark of royalty on his hand."

"The chiromantic hand".

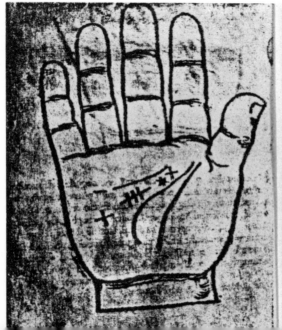
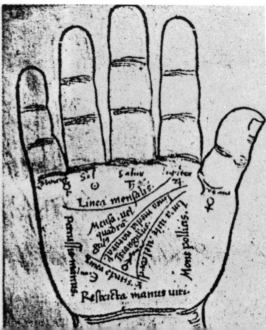

2. The physiognomy of the hand.

The chiromantic and chirognomic study of the hand may be divided into two parts: the study of the *shape* of the hand *(palm and fingers)*, or chirognomony, and the study of its lines, or chiromancy.

An individual's mental and physical balance can be assessed from the degree of harmony which exists between the palm and the fingers. The palm represents the personal faculties, the subjective elements in the brain, the individual traits which are characteristic of a person's mental outlook and also the resilience of his physical and moral health. The fingers indicate the manner in which one expresses one's thoughts, and, to use a term commonly found in chiromantic literature, the physical forms assumed by the "atavistic laws of temperament." In other words, they personify elegance, artistic propensities, etc . . . as well as the various froms of the psycho-physical temperament, the act of seizing and of touching.

It would seem that ordinary folk have fingers which are rarely, if ever, in harmony with the palm. At the other extreme, those whose sophistication borders on decadence tend to have elongated, excessively flexible fingers which are almost wholly lacking in consistency. The lives lived by our ancestors have left evidence of variations of impulse, gestures, movements and preferences, all of them still plainly visible in the hands of men today.

Captain d'Arpentigny, founder of modern chirognomy, distinguished between seven basic shapes, or chirognomic types, which are commonly used by all those who engage in the empirical study of the hand:

1) The *elementary hand*, or the hand with a big palm;

2) The *necessary hand,* shaped like a spade, a spatula or a carpet-beater;

3) The *artistic hand,* tapering and conical;

4) The *useful hand,* angular or square;

5) The *philosophical*, or knotted hand;

6) The *psychic*, or pointed hand;

7) The mixed hand, which is not really a type at all, but an intermediate shape.

1) The *elementary hand* is broad and thick; its strong, stout fingers are lacking in flexibility; the thumb is turned outwards; the palm is "too broad, too thick and too hard."

A hand such as this belongs to "coarse individuals" with a "slow imagination", and who are "lazy and indifferent."

2) The *necessary hand,* shaped like a spatula, has a "big" thumb, and the last phalange of each finger shaped like a "more or less blunt spatula". This hand belongs to "hard workers", "business people", "people with a good head for figures", "people whose lives are governed by arithmetic"; it is a sign of vigorous, decisive activity, and of persistent application to one's work.

In D'Arpentigny's own words, the spatulate, or spade-shaped, hand, with a big thumb, doubtless originated in regions where the harsh climate and relative barrenness of the soil made it more necessary than it would have been in the

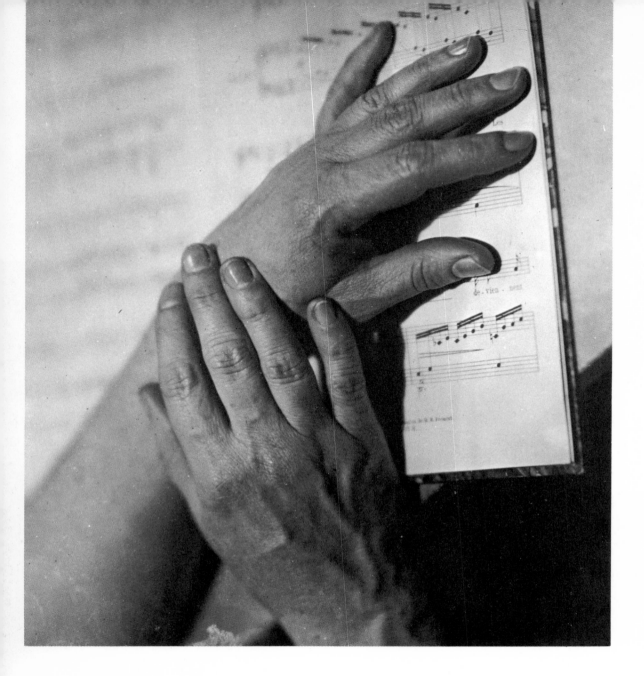

South for people to lead active lives, move about from one place to another, and practise those skills which help protect man's physical weakness from the rigors of his environment.

Spatulate hands are the hands of settlers, men who love the "material things of the soil." They are very mobile people. The practical aptitudes of the Americans stems precisely from the abundance of these working hands. Charles the Fifth of Spain owed his glory to the qualities which he found in Flemish hands: the hands of cold, hard-working, slow people who were quite unlike the imaginative and adventurous Spanish temperament. "Charles the Fifth chose precisely his Flemish subjects, with their big, square hands, to organise, administer, exploit and maintain his continued rule over the territories which he had conquered with his Spanish subjects, whose hands were dry and pointed."

D'Arpentigny was full of praise for spatulate

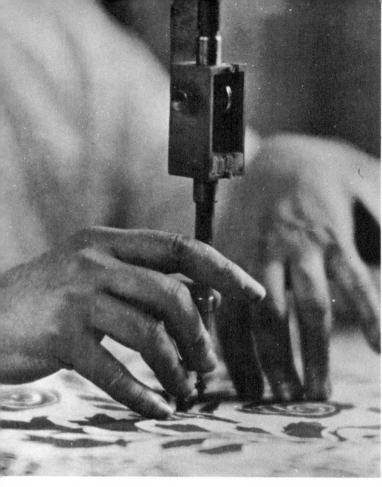

Craftsmen's hands, with their evident refinement and practical sense: a dressmaker, a potter, a painter (Fernand Léger). Reverse side: a cutler, a pastry cook, a bishop . . .

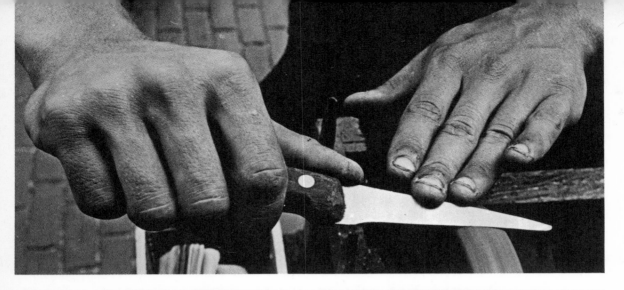
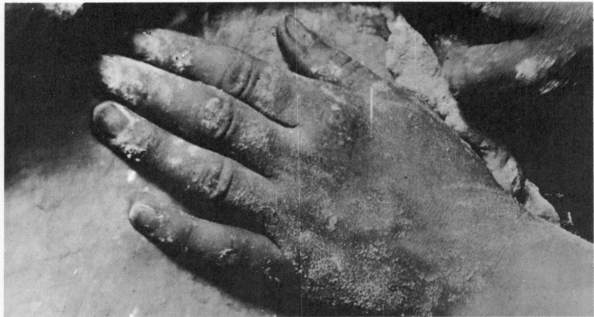
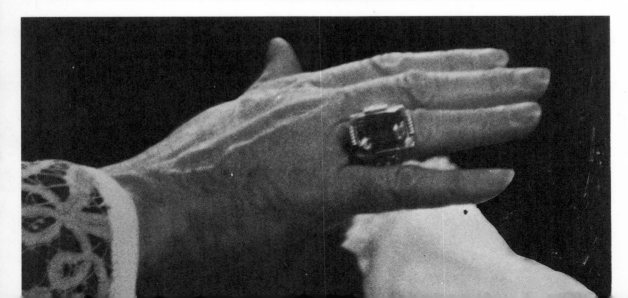

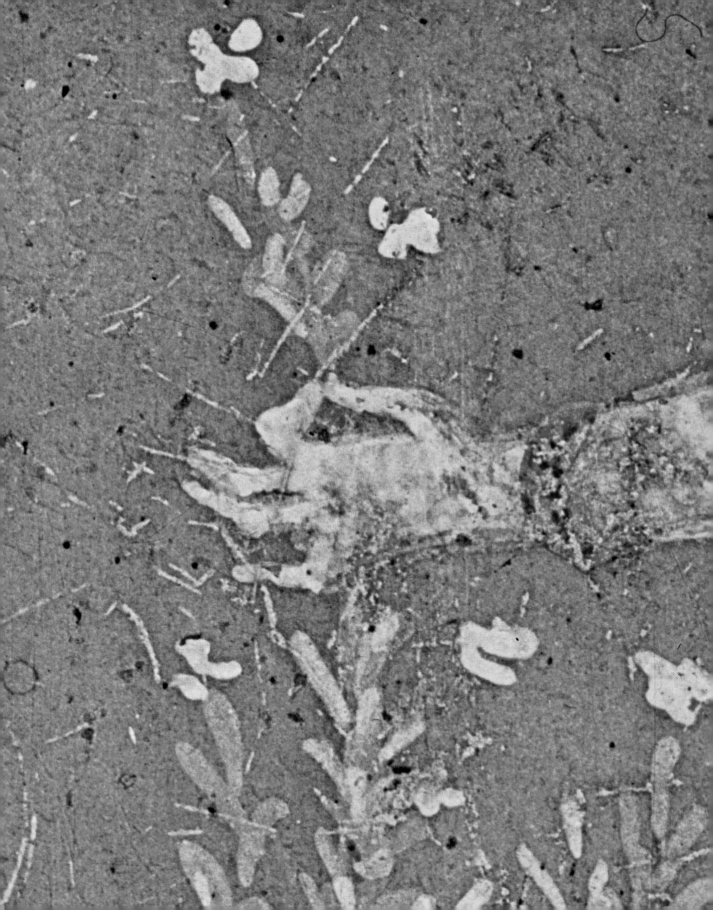

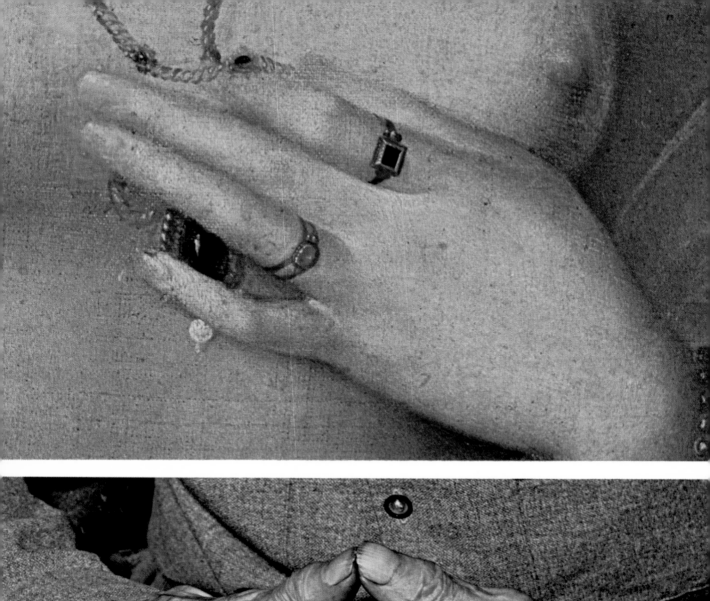

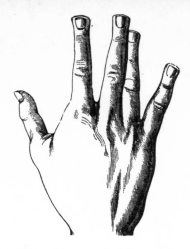

hands. Without them, he felt, a powerful and sound society would be out of the question. The hands of the Napoleonic admirers of the French Revolution—hardly a type D'Arpentigny would be likely to admire—all had spatula-shaped hands, as did the *petit caporal* himself. "Moreover", he wrote, "his hands, which have been extravagantly praised, were neither refined nor delicate: they were quite strong, stubby and thick."

3) The *artistic hand* can be distinguished mainly by the fact that only the fingers are pointed, while the palm and the rest of the hand seem to have quite normal proportions. The thumb is the criterion which determines the basic psychic type; and its shape may vary widely, and reflects a correspondingly wide variety of sub-types in this broad psychic category. According to D'Arpentigny, there are three main types: 1) a flexible hand, with a small thumb and

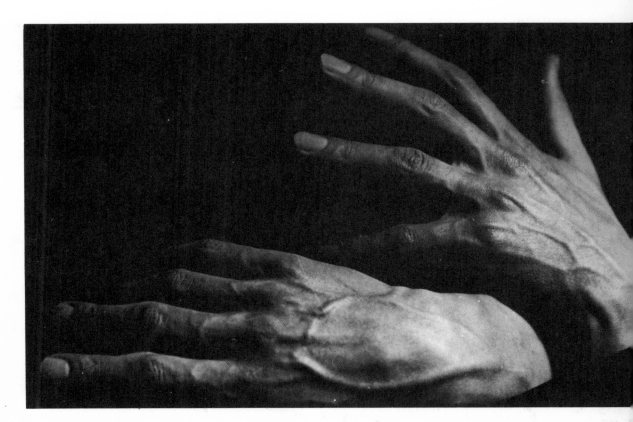

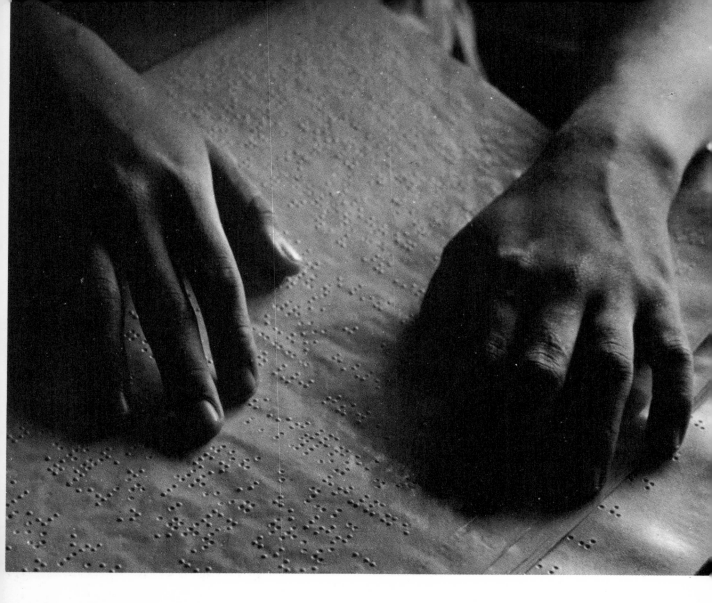

medium sized palm; 2) a flexible hand with a big thumb, and a broad, thick palm; and 3) a very firm, big hand, with a big palm. The first sub-type is an artistic hand, whose owner has a particular awareness of beauty of shape and line. The second sub-type is more material: the individual is more inclined towards financial dealings—an ambitious hand. The first sub-type is characterized by "enthusiasm", the second by deviousness, and the last by physical desire. Generally speaking, this third category is evidence of a fickle, impressionable mind, which, while capable of deep thought, is more likely to react in spontaneous bursts of enthusiasm.

In the opinion of D'Arpentigny, the fingers of the artistic hand are "voluminous for the length of the first phalange, gradually tapering thereafter down to the tip, which is shaped rather like a flattened cone. The thumb is small, and the palm well developed."

4) The *useful hand (square or angular)*, is a type which belongs to a methodical, well-ordered mind; it is often the hand of a solid, reliable employee, a thorough, painstaking civil servant, for example: an entirely unexceptional person, with a mediocre mind. This hand is more often large than small, with knotted fingers, a

medium-sized palm, and the final phalanges square rather than spatulate. One might say that this is the hand of a slave. "The thumb is big and has a well-developed base; the palm is of medium dimensions, hollow and quite firm". Referring to this intellectual category of men, D'Arpentigny had the following to say: "Such people can rarely lift their eyes above the level of the ground, which is where they truly belong. Their knowledge of the world of ideas is as limited as is the naked eye's perception of the heavens. They are quick to dismiss anything which they can neither feel nor understand; and fondly imagine that nature's boundaries lie exactly along the confines of their own narrow understanding."

5) The *philosophical hand* has broad, knotted fingers, and a broad, but supple, palm. The finger tips are neither square nor spatulate, but slightly oval, indeed almost conical. The thumb is big and is divided into two fairly equal halves by a clearly marked joint. The shape of the fingers of the philosophical hand indicates poetical sentimentality, together with an "intuitive sense of calculation," as Captain D'Arpentigny would put it, this trait being related to the knotted conformation of the fingers, and a capacity for rigorous, logically made deductions, which are related to the precise division of the thumb into equal halves. D'Arpentigny felt that the philosophical hand was a sign of the metaphysical instinct, or that of "acute criticism."

6) The *psychic hand* is exceptionally beautiful and rare. It is small and pleasant to touch; its gently undulating fingers are slender and smooth; the thumb is small and elegant, and its last phalange slightly longer than the other two.
Hands of this type belong to people who have

genuine intellectual gifts, who are clearly above their environment and who are motivated by noble, disinterested and idealistic purposes.

7) The *mixed hand* comprises those ill-defined types which belong to several of these categories, and yet can not be classified in any

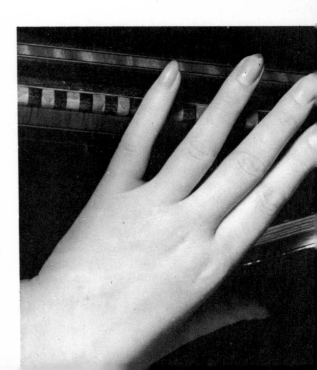

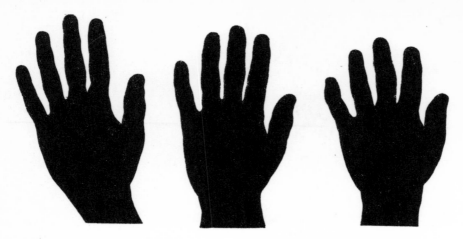

of them. These are intermediate types, lacking in special aptitudes of any sort.

As its name suggests, a mixed hand has something of each of the two types of intelligence indicated by its shape.

D'Arpentigny regarded these hands as the basic component of the moderating power of the masses.

3. The study of the hand in classical chiromancy.

The palm is the one part of the hand on which expert chiromantists focus their attention most sharply.

All chirognomic manuals recommend that examination of this part of the hand should proceed in the following manner:

1) its dimensions, 2) the degree of its firmness, 3) its internal color—a commonly used term, meaning the tactilo-muscular physiognomy of the palm.

The palm

A broad, firm, almost hard palm means an industrious person, with well defined personal ideas, often bordering on intransigence. Some would way that it also means: honesty, candor and a loyal character, while others would be more inclined to emphasize that such people lead very active intellectual and physical lives, and enjoy good health.

A palm which is broad but supple belongs to a mind capable of grasping general concepts; a spontaneous type of character. Some experts would add that it is evidence of vast knowledge,

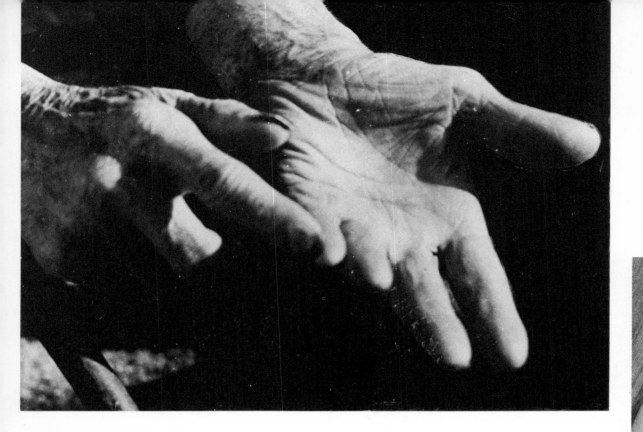

or a fondness for philosophical reasoning, and a preference for mental over physical activity; while others think it is the sign of a kind, helpful person, one who is anxious to be of service to others. It is thought by some to point to delicate, yet nonetheless fairly good health.

A very large and prominent palm, well out of proportion with the fingers, is a sign of violence and malice. It strongly suggests a dangerous, unbalanced person. Its opposite, a narrow slender palm, would mean narrowness of mind, and sluggish mental powers, vague, illogical ideas; a suspicious, headstrong person, quick to take offense; highly impressionable and almost incapable of frankness. A narrow palm which is strong is the physical sign of selfishness, sensuality and an irritable character.

A medium-sized, suppled and well-proportioned palm suggests mental balance, and, at the same time, the kind of health which, while not very robust, is nevertheless quite sound. The classics of chiromancy would say that it means the power to assimilate abstract knowledge, a lively, clear intelligence, sound judgment. A hard, coarse palm means a great amount of physical activity, a love of sports and movement: a violent disposition, and a total lack of sensitivity. If the palm is supple and firm, its owner will be a person of very refined sentiments; he will have a lively intelligence, which he will constantly seek to improve; he will possess the highest integrity. A very soft palm is a sign of laziness and voluptuous pleasure, an extremely hesitant will and very delicate health. Smooth, dry hands indicate ambition, positivism, ruthless greed together with pride and a capacity for taking offense rather easily. An authoritarian, domineering character, with devious ways; as likely as not, he will be a prey to digestive disorders. A thick, hard palm means a sensual, materialistic person; quarrelsome, with a strong will. A thick and soft palm: laziness, cowardice and inertia—the helpless plaything of instinct. The big hand is analytical, the medium-sized hand indicates a synoptic mind, while the very small type of hand suggests a mind capable of synthesis.

The fingers

The *fingers* are quite as important in chiromancy as the palm. They are to be studied in their entirety as well as in the details of their proportions; accordingly, each phalange must be considered with particular care, first of all as a separate entity, and then in comparison with the others.

The nail-bearing phalange, also known as the "first phalange," because of its dominant position, represents the pure cerebral functions. Thinkers, cultivated minds, and those who are commonly thought of as intellectuals usually have a first phalange which is longer than the others. According to the classics of our subject, meditation, a love of philosophy and the abstract sciences are indicated if the first phalange is mildly spatulate in shape. This category comprises people who "need physical motion," "action at any price," "love without tenderness," in other words, "audacious types," in the opinion of D'Arpentigny. However, minds which are truly prime movers, more spontaneous than logical, will usually be seen to have a somewhat conical finger-tip, which is almost pointed in the case of utopian theoreticians, inventors, or people given to exalted intuitive thinking. Spatulate, knotted fingers belong to people whose gifts lie more in the direction of the mechanical sciences, strategy, and also to talented instrumentalists: Liszt, for example, had huge hands, knotted fingers and very spatulate phalanges.

A square first phalange is evidence of common sense, a positive, methodical approach, simplicity, conformity, a love or order, a sense of organization, but does not indicate the ability to take initiatives.

The second phalange is a sign of the balance that exists between the ideal and the functional,

and shows the degree of an individual's sense of the practical. If it is longer than the others, powers of reasoning and notions of positive order prevail; but if it is short, illusions predominate, at the expense of common sense.

The third phalange represents the material sphere, sensual impressions and the more or less impetuous violence of the instincts. When thick, this phalange always indicates a voluptuous nature, which loves in indulge in the luxury of a comfort and a thoroughly idle existence; when dry or thin, it means that the individual in question is incurably hard-hearted and malevolent. When well-proportioned, it is evidence of an affectionate, kind, even devoted kind of person.

When the fingers, by comparison with the proportions of the palm, are long, broad and firm, they suggest an extremely well-adjusted, vigorous individual, a strong mind.

Long tapering fingers: excessive attention to detail, painstaking observation and analysis; refined tastes; sensitivity which may, at times, border on decadence; delicate health. These are the fingers of diplomats and sophisticates.

Long, spatulate fingers: pessimistic, irritable, sullen and suspicious character; complacent, fairly indifferent to others; harshly critical.

Medium fingers, nicely proportionate to the palm: well-adjusted, a quick, clear mind; good general grasp of knowledge.

Short stubby fingers: impulsive character; violent, thoughtless, hare-brained, rash, inconsistent.

Very short and very stubby fingers: cruelty, stubbornness.

Short, square fingers: a mind more given to synthesis than to analysis; a clear, active mind, good powers of reasoning loyalty and fidelity.

Short, pointed fingers: a liar, with an unba-

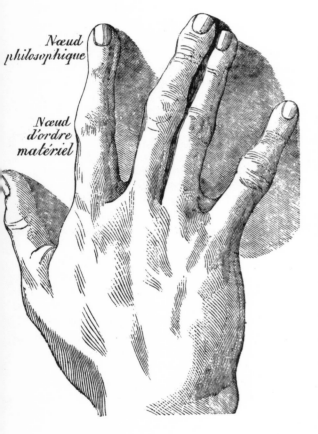

Nœud philosophique

Nœud d'ordre matériel

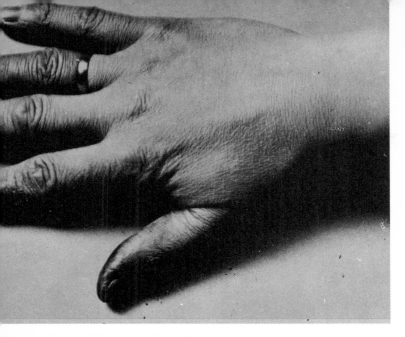

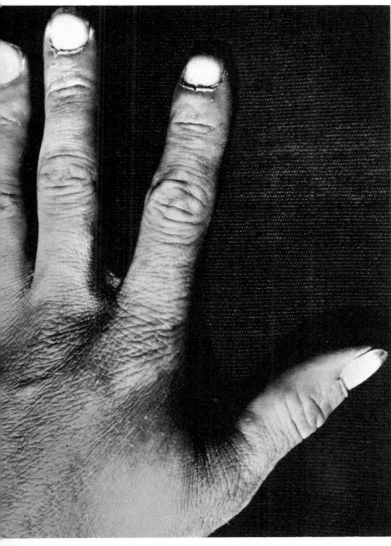

lanced imagination; selfish, and unable to formulate sound judgments.

Elegant, fleshy fingers, with a graceful slender root: highly self-centered, an absolute, almost a studied lack of awareness of the sufferings of others; a fondness for extreme comfort. Very much a type to be avoided.

Inelegant, but supple fingers, able to bend backwards: impulsive generosity, big—heartedness, altruism, an agile intellect, but a rather weak will.

Firm fingers, not rigid: lively, original intelligence; a person who knows exactly what he wants.

"Hooked" fingers are so well known as hardly to need a comment from us: they suggest a well-defined psychological type.

Hard fingers, which bend only with great difficulty: a lack of mental flexibility; an irritable person, given to quibbling; a caustic wit; lacking in generosity.

Stout, clumsy fingers belong to stolid, earthbound types, accustomed to hard physical toil. When shapeless, these fingers are strongly suggestive of coarse, nasty and frequently cruel types; if they are bent and misshapen, they belong to people of inferior intelligence. They are irritable, petty and ill-adjusted.

Chirognomony divides men into two categories, according to the appearance of their fingers: those with *smooth* fingers and those whose fingers are *knotted*. People belonging to the first of these categories are more inclined to be moved by intuition, spontaneous impressions, whims or artistic taste; whereas in the latter category one is more likely to find mature thought, logic, and a precise calculating intellect.

Descartes and Pascal had knotted fingers.

In both chiromancy and chirognomony, the

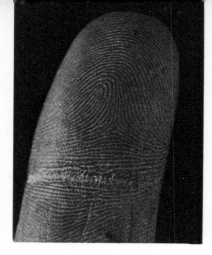

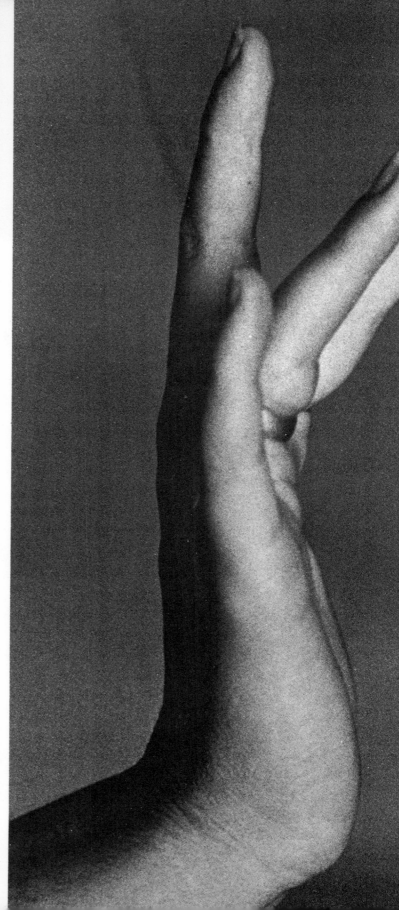

thumb constitutes a whole chapter apart. On account of its position, it is independent of the other fingers, which seem in fact to be under its control; in chiromantic studies, a curious and complex symbolism has always surrounded it, so much so that a disproportionately large amount of information may be gleaned from this one part of the hand.

The location of the thumb, opposite the fingers, is almost a distinctively human trait. A small thumb is a sign of an indecisive mind, whereas a big thumb is evidence of strength and authority. Voltaire, for example, had unusually big thumbs, as did Napoleon; in fact, both of these cases are frequently quoted in the literature of chirognomony.

At birth, the thumb is almost always hidden and folded under the other fingers; as the child grows it gradually assumes a more personal role, when it opens and begins to move. During sleep, the thumb reverts to the folded position it occupied in its first days; the same kind of reversion occurs at the moment of death, when it disappears under the other fingers, once more adopting the folded position of the thumb of a newborn child. This reflex is thought to be the sign of the termination of personality. One may conclude therefore that the liveliness of a person's mind varies directly with the degree of detachment between the thumb and the other fingers. When it lies close to the index finger, on an inflexible hand, it suggests a lower, uncultivated type of mind. However, when it is flexible and points unmistakably outwards, it is a sign of flexibility of mind and character, of generosity and magnanimity.

The first, or nail-bearing phalange of the thumb is almost the only indication one needs in order to discern the qualities of energy, decisiveness

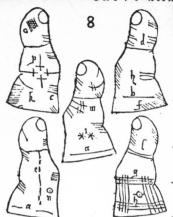

8

BI habundè satis de literis diuinis & de charaꞔeribus, qui in montibus planetarum aliquã do inueniri poſſunt, traꞔatum eſt : ad digitos nũc meritò pro- cedendum eſt , qui etiam ſuos particulares habent charaꞔe- res , & de eorum ſignificatio- nibus dicendum reſtat. Et pri- mò de pollice, qui eſt diꞔus di- gitus Veneris, eò quod monti Veneris ſuperemiꞔet , qui ſi ſit colore viuo,et rubenti benè di ſpoſitus,bonam corporis quali- tatem notat,& mulierũ ama- torem oſtendit hominem , ve- ſtitus pulchros appetentem,& munditijs ſtudentem. Quod ſi in eo breuiuſcula alia linea , ſecundum vit.e lineam reꞔè diuoluatur , vt in li-

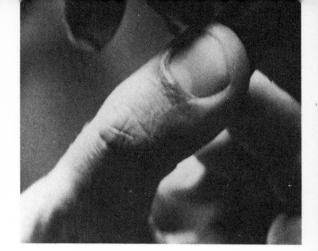

and activity in a person. When this phalange is much longer than the second phalange, it is a sign of extreme stubbornness; when medium, it means moderate but constant will-power, a thoughtful person; when short, weakness; and when very short and sloping sharply backwards, it means that the person's character is marred by the flaw of positivism, impressionability, indif- ference and an incoherent will.

The following observations apply to the sec- ond phalange:

Long: prudence, acute power of analysis, lack of spontaneity.

Medium: wisdom, integrity and common sense.

Short: thoughtlessness, a capacity for foolish impulsive acts.

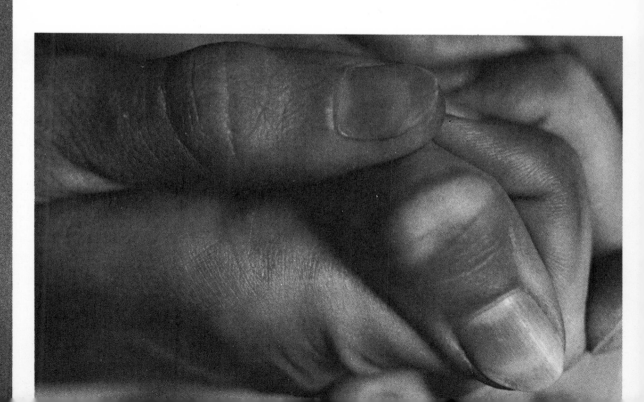

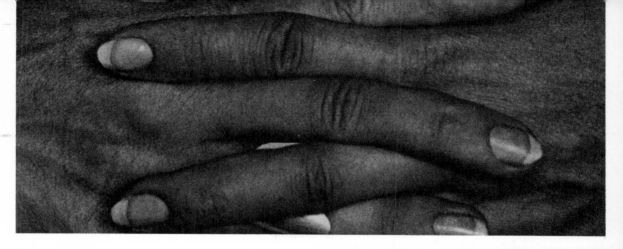

The mounts

The mounts are situated on the palm, at the base of each finger, and are named after that finger. They are the Mount of Jupiter, of Saturn, of the Sun, of Mercury, and are arranged in the manner shown in the illustration. A particularly pronounced mount may attract a neighboring mount towards it, thereby creating one single mount in place of two, as sometimes happens with the organs in phrenology; the observer should then take into account the greater influence of the dominant attractive mount. The Mounts of Mars, the Moon and Venus are situated as follows:

The Mount of Mars begins below the Mount of Mercury, demarcated by the Heart Line; the Mount of Mars and the Mount of the Moon occupy two equal areas, the Mount of Mars coming first, and then the Mount of the Moon, which descends as far as the rascette line.

The Mount of Venus occupies the base of the thumb in the palm, where it looks like a sort of third phalange, although the thumb, in fact, has only two phalanges.

There is a school of thought which holds that the true basis of chiromancy is the study of the astral signatures. A 19th-century illustration will give the reader a clearer picture of them. It will ✫ 1 be found on the opposite page.

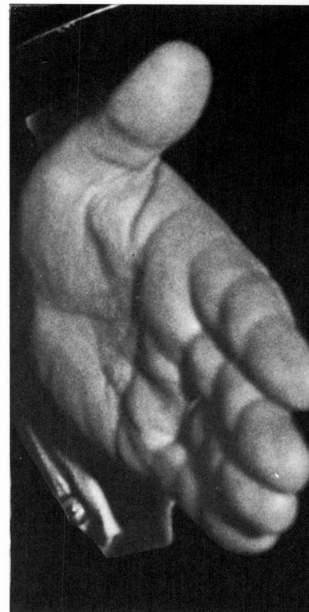

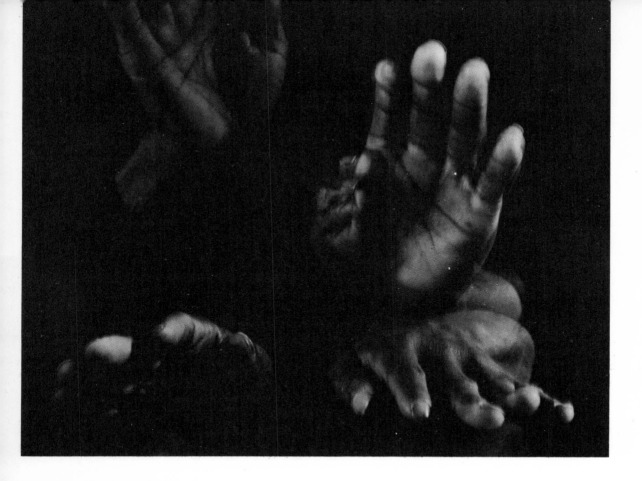

On the *Mount of Jupiter* (index finger) the picture represents royalty: ambition, pride and worldly honors.

The *Mount of Saturn* (middle finger) is shown as being related to mining; Saturn is thought to impart an aptitude for mining, prospecting and agriculture. The personal qualities it is associated with are independence and melancholy. The chiromantists of ancient times regarded it as a representative of fate.

The *Mount of the Sun* (ring finger) has Apollo, with his lyre. The sun confers on people an aptitude for the arts, peace of mind, dignity, a spirit of justice and clarity of thought.

The *Mount of Mercury* (little finger) is the lawyer. Mercury gives eloquence, diplomacy, business ability, skill, deviousness.

The *Mount of Mars* is the mount which shows Spartacus holding a sword; it expresses the warlike spirit, physical and moral energy, and, in general, the will to resist and attack (the picture of Spartacus should be placed on the same line as the battle which is supposed to take place only in the middle of the plain of Mars, in the middle of the palm).

The *Mount of the Moon*, symbolized by the sea, signifies a long sea-voyage to far-off places, as well as dreams, poetry, imagination, inconstancy. The appearance of the moon is itself constantly changing. In music, it represents harmony.

The *Mount of Venus*, designated by the lovers, is the mount of love, a taste for form in art, architecture and sculpture, and for style in literature; it also is also associated with the soul, with tenderness, kindness, charity and grace, and, in music, with melody.

The drawings which can be seen along the Life Line show, by means of the positions of the cradle, the adolescent, the young man, the grown man, the middle aged man, the old man and the grave, the various ages through which human life passes.

For the chiromantist, the thumb is vitally im-

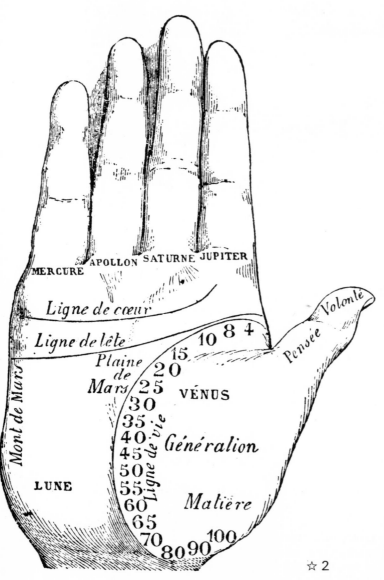

☆ 2

portant, because it represents will and logic. Logic, situated on the second phalange, is carrying a type of bullhorn, in order that its advice may be all the more easily heard by the *will*, which, from its position on the first phalange, in a commanding posture, is issuing orders to Saturn (fate).

The bracelet in the engraving represents the rascette lines, which some people also call the *magic bracelet.*

The following observations should also be noted:

Highly developed mounts mean an *excess* of the aptitudes proper to each mount.

Mounts which are *developed*, but not excessively so, mean a perfect level of the corresponding aptitude.

Mounts which are only faintly discernible indicate rather poor levels of aptitude.

Flat mounts are evidence of no aptitude at all.

When the mounts are *hollow*, rather than protruding, they signify the exact opposite of aptitude.

However, the *streaks*, which represent electricity, impart nervous energy to quite insignificant, even absolutely flat mounts.

Lines and signs ☆ 2

The principal lines of the hand are:

1) The Life Line, which circles the base of the thumb.

2) The Head Line, which crosses the middle of the hand.

3) The Heart Line, which runs next to the mounts at the base of the fingers.

However, all the other lines and each of the signs which occur in the hand also have their own special importance.

This very essential part of our subject is dealt with in the following chapters.

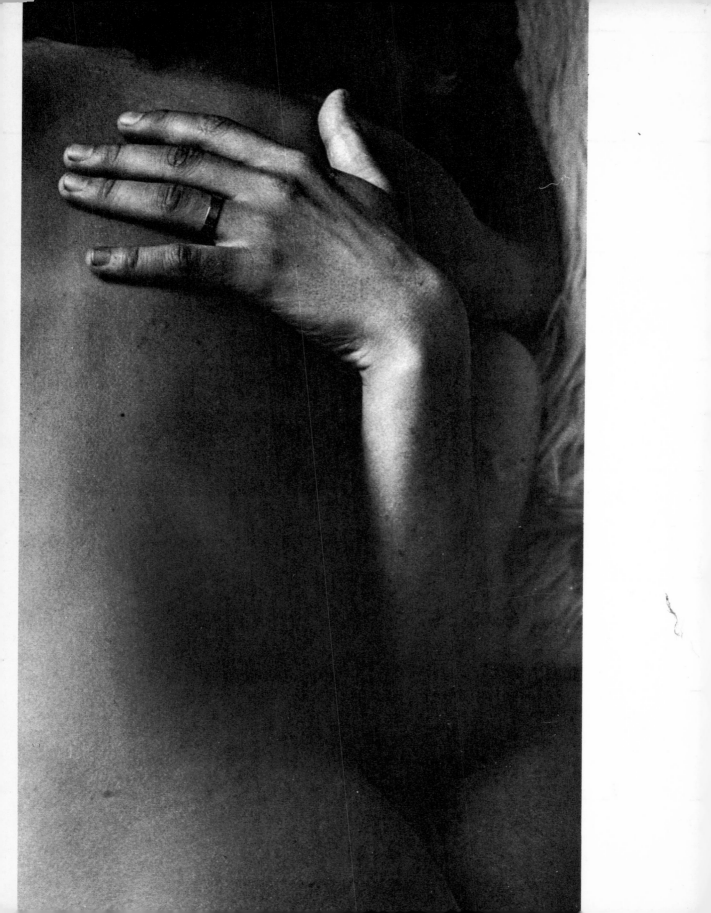

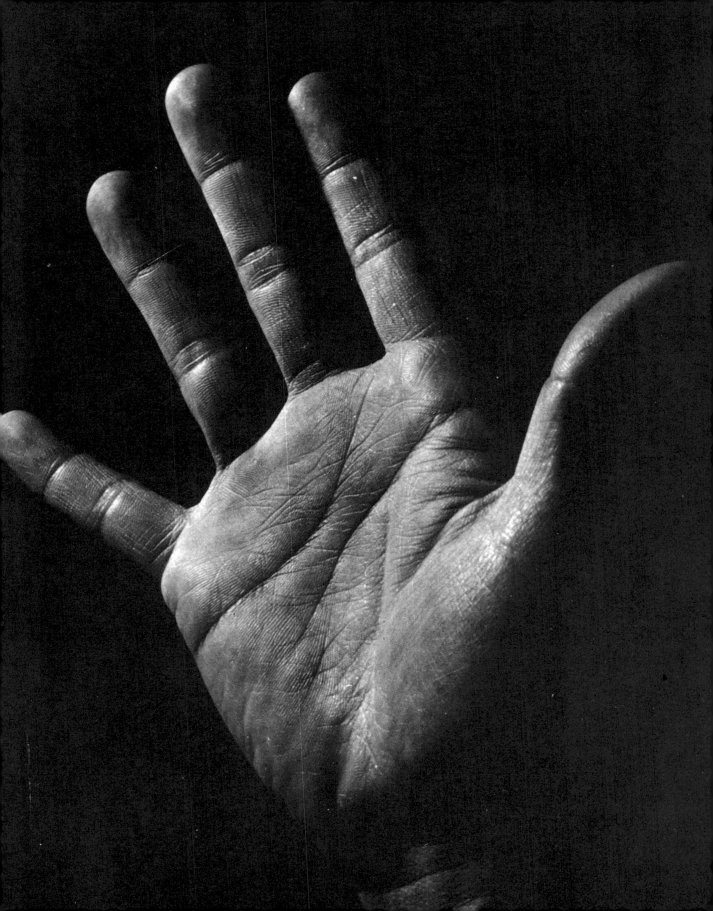

Advice from an expert: "The skin and the lines should be examined with a magnifying glass, in a well-lit room, preferably in sunlight. The examination should take place at moderate room-temperature, the subject should have refrained from any undue exertions or other excesses immediately before it, and, if possible, he should be fasting.« As for the Life Line, "this line should be most thoroughly scrutinized, so that none of its features—shape, color, length, depth, etc.—are overlooked. All measurements must be made with scrupulous care, and with the aid of a compass."

4. The principal lines of the hand

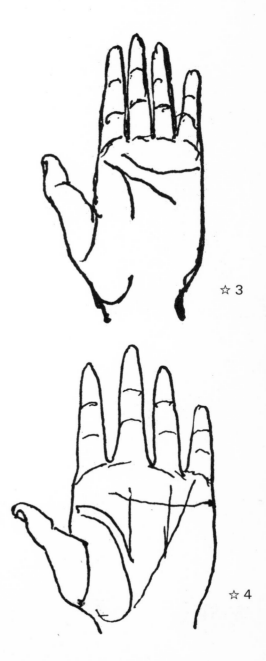

☆ 3

☆ 4

The Life Line

The Life Line, which runs around the base of the thumb, may under certain conditions, signify a long, happy life, free from illnesses, and also as well as a calm, resigned character. Those conditions are the following: it must be long and un-broken, without stains of various colors, without cross-bars, without stars, without islanded formations and without cuts—in other words, it must be a smooth, well-traced line, running around the thumb (such a perfect Life Line is rare, but is sometimes found).

The Life Line can tell us of the presence of disease in our life, and even, through an examination of the color and shape of the lines, the time when our health will come under attack.

☆ 3   When the Life Line is pale, it is a sign of delicate health, and a generally lymphatic organism.

If a Life Line is short, it indicates a life which is also short; if the line is the same in both hands, death will occur at the age at which the line stops.

Proper care, and, most particularly, the desire to live, can help one prolong one's life. In such cases, fine capillary lines form after the end of the Life Line, continuing the general direction of

☆ 4   the line, and deepening with advancing age.

If a short Life Line is accompanied by another

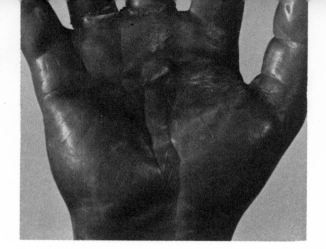

The hand of a murderer (Musée de la Préfecture de Police, Paris)

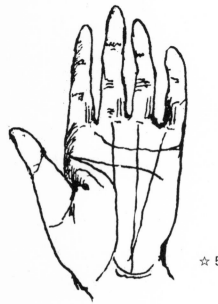

☆ 5

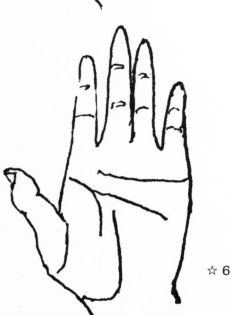

☆ 6

line which follows the direction of the first, within the mount of the thumb (the line of Mars), and reaches further down, this second line replaces the first and continues the life; a double Life Line means a long life. ☆ 5

If the hepatic line, which we shall describe later on, is particularly well formed, it replaces the Life Line. The hepatic line which runs from the rascette line to the Mount of Mercury indicates a very good stomach, and a perfect stomach preserves and prolongs one's life; the person's strength will decline during the period in which the Life Line may be broken or interrupted, but this is often quite harmless. Once this period has passed, health will be restored. When a double Life Line is accompanied by a well formed hepatic line, the individual's health will be remarkably good and his life will be long. ☆ 6

When the Life Line ends and merges with the Fate Line (Saturn), this latter line replaces or at least continues the Life Line. It can be said that there is a large element of luck in the person's continued existence; yet he may live just as long and as well as anyone else, even so.

If the Life Line is broken in one hand only, it is a sign of a serious illness occurring about the time of the break—in fact, the kind of illness for which doctors admit that they can do nothing; however, if the line continues in the other hand, the disease which was thought to be fatal will invariably be cured. Many cases of this phenomenon have occurred; patients who have been told by the specialists that they are doomed regain their spirits rapidly when re-assured in this way about their recovery, and their cure itself has indeed been accelerated by this knowledge.

A Life Line which consists of a series of chains is a sign of poor health or nervous disorders persisting throughout much of a person's life.

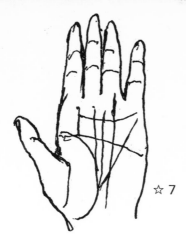 ☆ 7

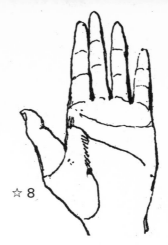 ☆ 8

Suffocatio.

1 *Pallidam lineam à radice indicis versus pollicem, suffocationem genti filij dicunt significare: hoc affirmat Antiochus.* **2** *Lineam vitæ inter indicem & pollicem tumentem, suffocationem partus, seu alterius infantis dicunt significare.* **3** *Mensalis in superiori parte bifurcata, & pallore suffusa, infantis mortem significat causa genitricis seu nutricis.*

DE DIVERSIS MORBIS ET AEGRI-
tudinibus, Caput XXII.

1 *Litera A in monte manus, varias ac diversas ægritudines notat.* **2** *Characteres Saturni in monte medij, ægritudinum multitudinem denunciant.*
3 *Linea à concauo extendens ramum ad brachium similem radio, ægritudinem intra sex annos, eiusdem lineæ partes si sint grossiores versus côcauum, quàm sunt circa brachium, infra duos annos denotat.*

4 *Lineæ paruæ iuxta radicem mensalis, ægritudines in prima ætate demonstrant, iuxta medium, in media ætate, iuxta finem, in vltima.* **5** *Linca ru-*

When the Life Line sends an offshoot from its point of departure to the Mount of Jupiter, you may expect to find an ambitious and often highly successful person. Many cases have been observed in which these offshoots have made a sudden appearance, thereby announcing some forthcoming success or the achievement of some ambition.

When the Heart Line joins the Head Line at the beginning of the Life Line, and all three lines merge into one, this is a fatal sign, meaning sudden violent death, which may, however, take place at quite an advanced age. It is also the sign of a serious accident.   ☆ 7

Smooth, unbroken and well-formed offshoots of the Life Line are always favorable, and usually indicate achievements founded on personal merit.   ☆ 8

Small gaps in the Life Line represent a period of poor health, occurring at the point in a person's life to which their position on the line corresponds.

A spot on the Life Line indicates an illness, and, in many cases, an injury; if the spot is deep and blackish, the injury in question may threaten the person's life, if it has not already done so.

If the Life Line is hollow throughout its length, it is a sign of violence or, at least, of rough behavior. If the line is slender, it means a melancholy temperament and a delicate constitution.

Illnesses and accidents show up on the Life Line in the form of a bluish patch which can be seen on the line at the age at which the illness is to occur. A black and blue patch is almost always a sign of a nervous disorder or brain trouble. A similar, blackish patch is commonly found on the Head Line, or, less frequently, the Heart Line.   ☆ 9

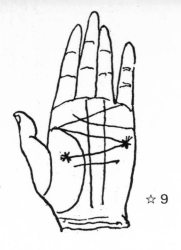

☆ 9

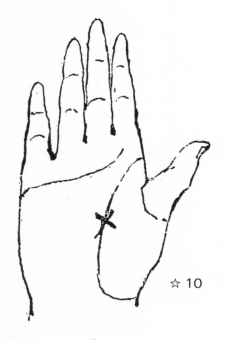

☆ 10

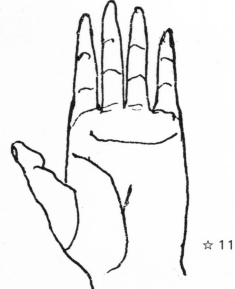

☆ 11

Illness resulting from some great emotional upset appears in the form of a line leading from the Mount of Venus, crossing the Life Line and continuing into the Plain of Mars. It almost invariably ends in the form of a point on the Head Line or the Heart Line. All lines which run from the Mount of Venus, across the Life Line, and into the palm mean emotional distress, or a threat to a person's position in the world. If these lines go further and cross the Fate Line, or merge into a cross on that line, they always mean a threat to a person's wealth. When they end in a star on the Head Line, it is a portent of great misfortunes which may even upset the balance of the mind. When this line intersects the Sun Line, both rank and fortune are threatened. This is a line which is most commonly found at the beginning of a person's life. It often reflects a loss of wealth caused by misfortunes such as a financial collapse experienced by one's parents. The relevant age is always indicated by the position at which the line crosses the Life Line.

It frequently happens that this loss is caused by the death of a parent: such a death would be indicated by a star on the Mount of Venus which would mark the point of departure of the line indicating financial collapse or some violent emotional distress, such as the death of a spouse or even of a friend. This is particularly so when these deaths have disastrous consequences for one's worldly position or wealth. ☆ 10

A cross on the Life Line is an event which was fated to happen; a forked offshoot which does not cut across the Life Line shows the time in a person's life at which an illness occurs; if the fork ☆ 11 and the area immediately around it are dark, the illness will be serious and will be due to nervous irritation. Illnesses related to gout bear these markings. ☆ 12

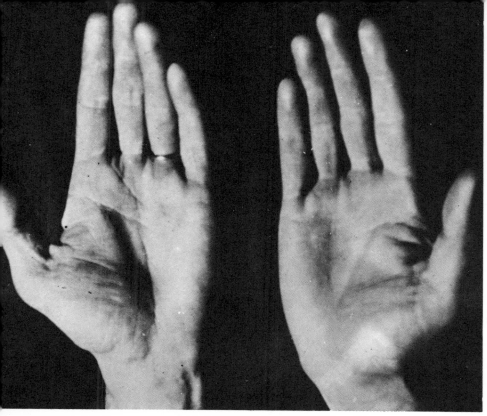

The lines of the left and right hands are often quite different: the first is the hand of destiny, and the second is the hand of will. The first cannot be interpreted without an examination of the second, which will confirm it, or, more commonly, correct or aggravate it.

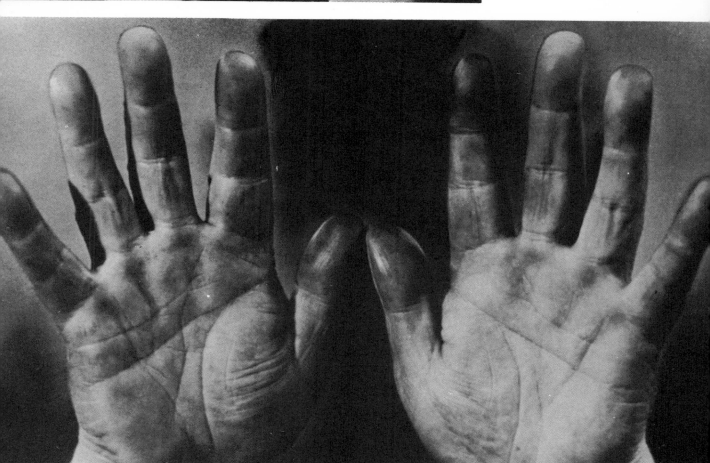

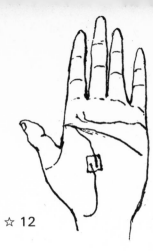

☆ 12

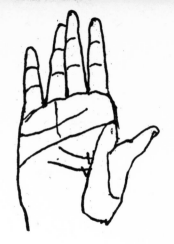

☆ 13

☆ 13 A Life Line broken into two sections—as long as the distinct parts are, as it were, framed by a square—is a sign of a terrible disease, the effects of which will be reversed by the square, which represents preservation, of whatever sort. Wherever this square occurs, and particularly if it surrounds lines which appear to pose a threat to health or worldly position, it means recovery. If the observer notes this sign at a point relating to the past, he will recall that at the period in question, he had avoided some danger or other thanks to help from an unexpected quarter.

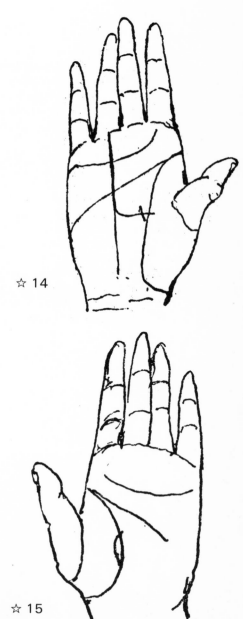

☆ 14

☆ 14 If the Life Line has a small fork, intersected by a line of grief which thereby forms a kind of cross, it means that legal action will be taken, and, as often as not, that a marriage will break up. If the point of departure of this line on the Mount of Venus is a star, it means that legal proceedings will take place involving parents, friends or one's relatives and associates, in connection, for example, with a dispute over an inheritance, or a bankruptcy. In cases where this line continues and crosses the Sun Line, one should expect to find a severe loss in a court case, capable of causing financial ruin.

☆ 15 However, this fatalistic sign sometimes ends at the Sun Line in the Plain of Mars, that is, in the quadrangle situated in the middle of the palm; if the line in question merges with the Sun Line, without actually crossing it, the court case will not merely be won, but will also produce significant gains for the subject.

If an islanded formation occurs in the Life Line, it should be interpreted as meaning illness or depression throughout the period represented by the size of the formation on the Life Line. The state of the Heart Line and the Head

☆ 15

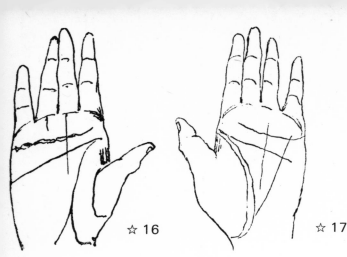

☆ 16   ☆ 17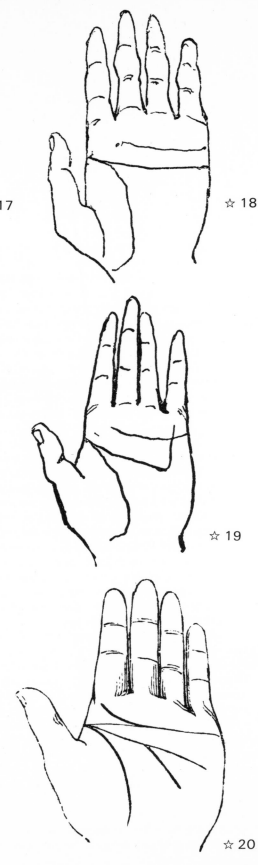

☆ 18

Line, as well as any excess in the mounts, in-dicates the type of illness. If the hepatic line is missing or poorly formed, stomach disorders or migraines are likely to occur. Such stomach dis-orders or migraines may respond favorably to violent exercise, such as fencing or canoeing, which helps the subject sweat a lot; the illness it-self will not be eliminated, but its more painful manifestations will be prevented.

Islands on the Life Line at the age which women refer to as the "critical age" are a sign of various afflictions and sufferings about this time.   ☆ 16

In men, at the point corresponding to middle age, the Life Line forks, which means a dispersal of the sap of life. This is not an illness in the strict sense of the term, but merely a lessening of one's strength, and a warning signal about the dangers of too much work. Particular care should be taken only when one's energy is visibly waning; judicious relaxation should then enable one to start again with extra vigor.   ☆ 17

☆ 19

When the Life Line curls around as so as to form a semi-circle with the point of departure (birth), this is a sign of a long life, which may, if the hepatic line is good, exceed a hundred years.

It is important to remember that the line which accompanies the Life Line, and which we call the Line of Mars, its sister line, in fact, repairs the damage due to the accidents, flaws, and ill-nesses indicated on the Life Line.

☆ 20

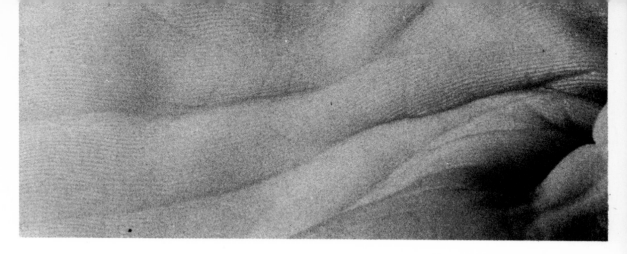

The Head Line

The Head Line begins between the thumb and the index finger and is normally joined to the Life Line for a part of its length; after a while, they diverge, the Head Line following any one of a number of courses, while the Life Line runs around the base of the Mount of Venus.

If it does not go beyond the middle of the Mount of Mercury, the Head Line signifies reason and clarity of thought. ☆ 18

If it proceeds horizontally across the palm as far as the percussion, or edge of the palm, it is evidence of a good grasp of business, positive thinking, egotism, greed, ruthlessness, and even a cold, calculating approach, if the fingers are smooth. No matter how it may be modified by various other lines, a well-traced Head Line of this type is always evidence of at least a strong basic sense of economy. This Head Line belongs particularly to the moral predator—even more so when it curves upwards to form a crease on the Mount of Mercury: in this case, it means that the person is extremely crafty and devious in his business dealings, and that his conscience conveniently moves to one side whenever there is a possibility that it may stand in the way of profits. ☆ 19

Business people of this sort usually have a Head Line with two branches, one of which climbs towards the Mount of Mercury, while the other presses on inexorably, dividing the hand in two. ☆ 20

A Head Line which forks at the end into two branches—one going straight and the other descending slightly towards the Mount of the Moon, indicates a propensity for double standards, pretexts and, where necessary, lies: lawyers, sophists and, in general, those engaged in the legal profession are likely to have this kind of hand. The same forked line is common in the hands of great actors, who have to forget their own personality in order to embrace that of the character whose part they are playing on stage. This fork is particularly common in the hands of clever women; its influence will vary directly according to the degree of development of the Mount of Mercury. ☆ 21

If, after crossing the Plain of Mars, the Head Line, instead of going straight, descends towards the Mount of Moon, it denotes a penchant for poetry and imagination. If it goes even further down, reaching the rascette line, though still on the Mount of Moon, it denotes a love of the oc-

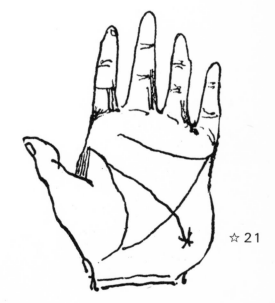

☆ 21

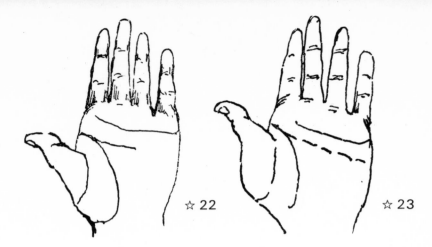

☆ 22   ☆ 23

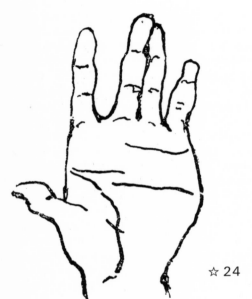

☆ 24

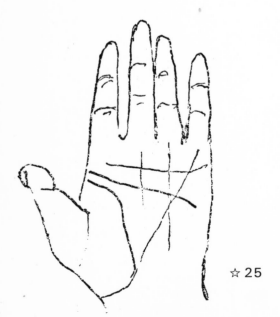

☆ 25

cult, superstition and clairvoyance; this kind of spiritualism can, if the Head Line reaches far down the hand and ends in a star, lead to madness. If this line slopes only towards the Mount of Moon, and if this mount has a number of creases, in a criss-cross pattern near the rascette, it means that the person is fond of poetry and literature.

If the Head Line forms a big cross as it meets the hepatic line on the Mount of Moon, it signifies a person with exalted ideas. ☆ 22

If the Head Line stops below Saturn, it is a sign of death, an early death, or of a threat to one's intelligence. When the Head Line goes no further than the middle of the hand, it means a fairly low level of intelligence, or at least incoherence and lack of intellectual staying power, and an untidy, shallow mind. ☆ 23

If the Head Line is made up of short truncated sections, the person in question frequently suffers from headaches, and has fits of forgetfulness, which are sometimes so bad that he cannot complete an idea he has begun to express, or even finish a sentence. ☆ 24

When the Head Line is broken into two super-imposed segments, just below Saturn, it denotes a grave injury, perhaps to the head, or a broken limb, in which case the leg is more likely to be involved than the arm. This sign is often found in one hand only. ☆ 25

When the Head Line is separated from the Life Line, it represents great self-confidence, uncontrollable outbursts of frankness, rash decisions taken on the spur of the moment, on a wave of enthusiasm, and passions which are, in the context, singularly dangerous. The advice that should be given to a person bearing this sign in his hand is that, unless it is clearly to his advantage to act otherwise, he should exercise enor-

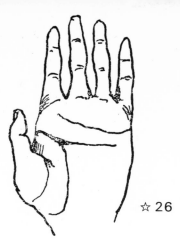
☆ 26

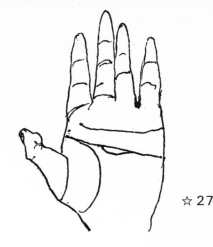
☆ 27

mous self-restraint, always waiting another day before coming to a decision, in order to avoid disappointment or worse. A separate Head Line, occurring in a hand in which the planets Mars and Saturn are predominant, is a sign of boldness, indeed of sheer recklessness. This is the hand of impulsive, intuitive, headstrong people, these being traits commonly found in actors, lawyers, virtuoso concert artistes and opera singers. Such a hand gives them the kind of self-assurance which enables them to ignore the audience and maintain an absolutely unruffled composure. It is also very good for off-the-cuff speakers; they not only preserve their self-control, but relish in the sheer brilliance of their performance, for its own sake. As they sense their growing command of their audience, they allow their enthusiasm to sweep them along, with a dazzling display of bold, exciting ideas which often win the acceptance of the audience by virtue of their impetus alone. Almost all great court-room lawyers have a separate Head Line. This is the sign which Montaigne used to associate with loose women; the fact is that they are loose only when they have no force with which to resist a violent passion or overwhelming instincts.

☆ 26

Conversely, if the Head Line is joined to the Life Line and follows the same path for some distance, it denotes great timidity and lack of self-confidence; indeed, these qualities can often be quite overpowering. People with this sign and these traits, and who are clearly intelligent and industrious should be constantly encouraged to rid themselves of these morbid feelings of uncertainty and shyness.

Unless they have committed some act of outright folly, people with a separate Head Line *almost* always succeed, even if they are not particularly intelligent, whereas those whose Head Line lies too close to the Life Line succeed late in life, whether they do it on their own merits or find a protector—or they do not succeed at all. Everyone whose hand bears this sign can testify to the truth of this revelation themselves.

The Heart and Head Lines, while indicating disease, as well as the nature and seriousness of the disease, can give no idea of the timing of the disease without the help of the Life Line. It is true that, since the length of the Head Line does represent the span of a human life, one can get a rough idea of the point in a person's life at which a disease will occur or has occurred. But the Life Line is the only way to determine the moment precisely, by means of a line corresponding to the black or bluish patch which indicates the disease on the Line of Head. At that same spot, the Life Line has a black, or sometimes a bluish mark, or a break, if the illness is highly dangerous; sometimes there is a dot, if an injury is involved. Sometimes a transversal capillary line stretches from the Life Line to the sign which appears in the Head Line, in order to explain more fully the period and nature of the illness. ☆ 27

An island in the Head Line denotes nervous headaches which persist for the time represented by the length of the island.

A black or bluish spot in the Life Line indicates a typhoid or nervous fever, or extreme headaches for the period represented by the length of the mark on the line.

A hollow or dent in the Head Line indicates violent neuralgic pains lasting for at least one month a year, and often longer. ☆ 28

A star on the Head Line itself means either a serious head injury, or madness. ☆ 29

A star at the end of the Head Line, at the intersection of the hepatic line which leads to the Mount of Mercury, is always a sign of a dangerous or at least a painful childbirth; if a black

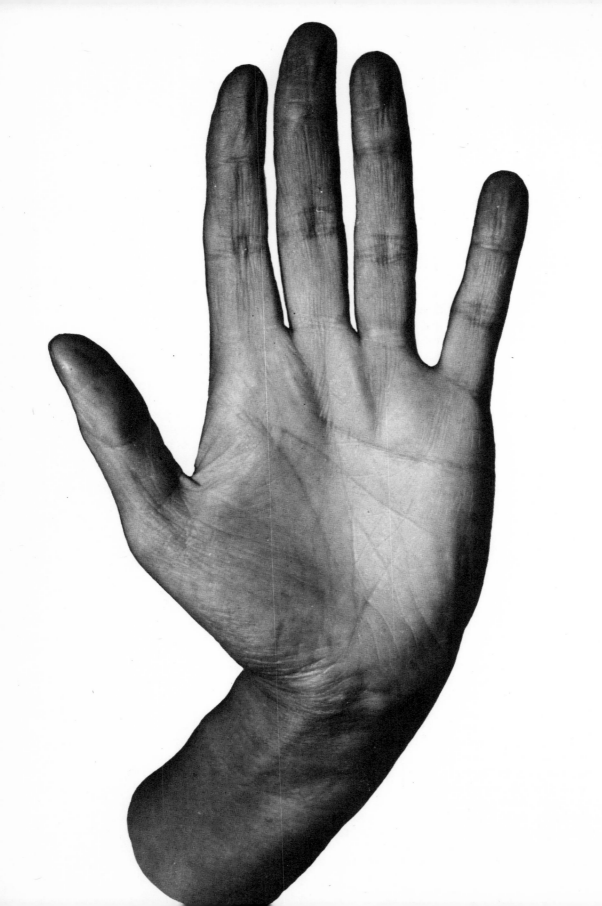

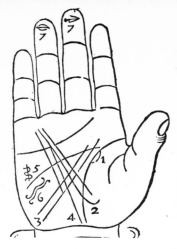

In 1653, Saunders, the English chiromantist, gave a detailed explanation of the signs and lines of this hand. Sign 1: "in a child's hand, this sign indicates that the child will be strangled or eaten by worms". Sign 6: death by drowning.

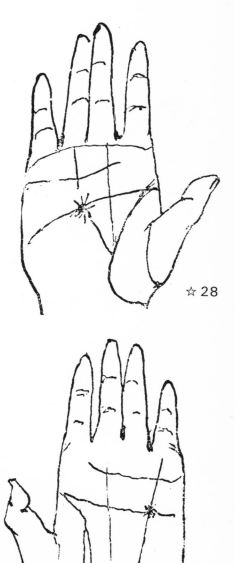

☆ 28

☆ 29

dot is visible at the same place, delirium may ensue. A well traced star means dangerous childbirth or sterility; what it means is that the organ is either inactive, thus making the delivery painful, or inert, in which case the woman is sterile.

Dark spots can also mean nervous pains in the teeth, ears and eyes, the type of disorder being indicated by the identity of the most pronounced mount. In this way, Saturn gives toothaches (bad teeth being one of the principal signatures of Saturn), and, when combined with a pronounced Mount of Venus, it gives deafness. The Sun-type gives disorders of the eyes, and indicates them by a star situated high on the Mount of Sun near the joint of the finger. In the lines, a dark yellowish color is a sign of liver disease; dark patches indicate nervous disorders; blue patches indicate the most serious organic illnesses, those least likely to respond to treatment.

A thin Head Line, faintly traced, just like the

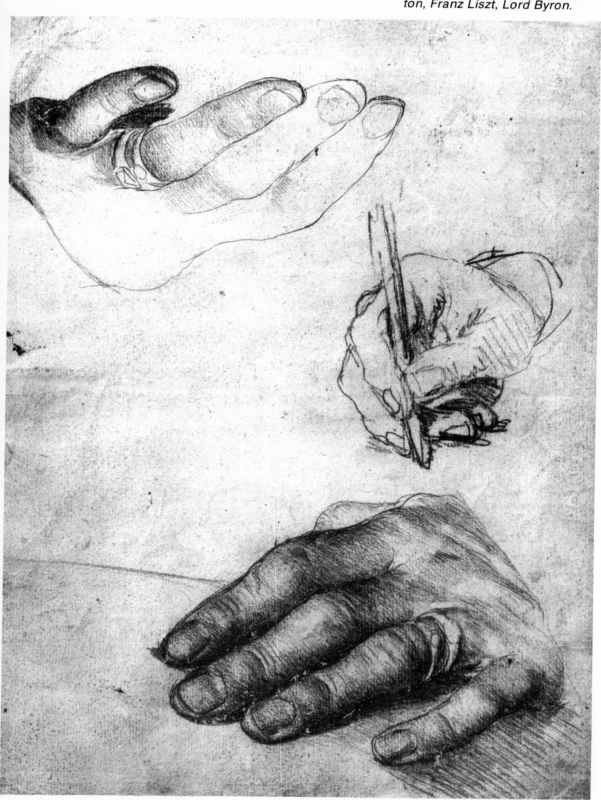

Famous hands: 1. Studies of the hand of Erasmus, by Holbein. 2. Andrea Doria, George Washington, Franz Liszt, Lord Byron.

54

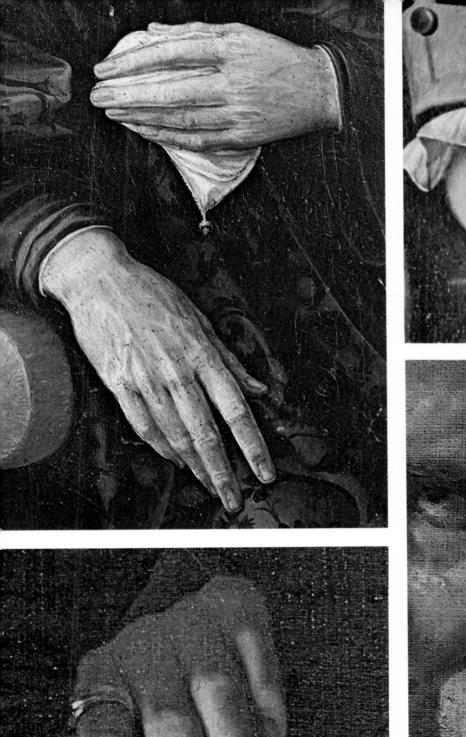
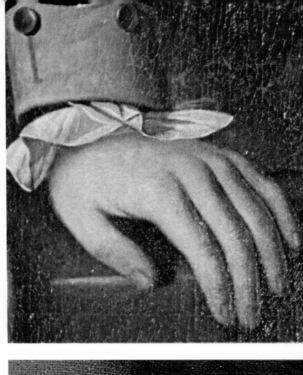
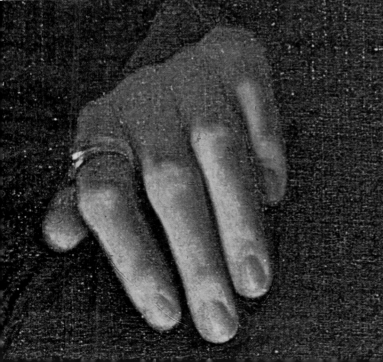
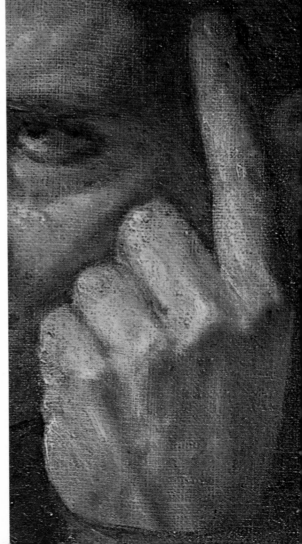

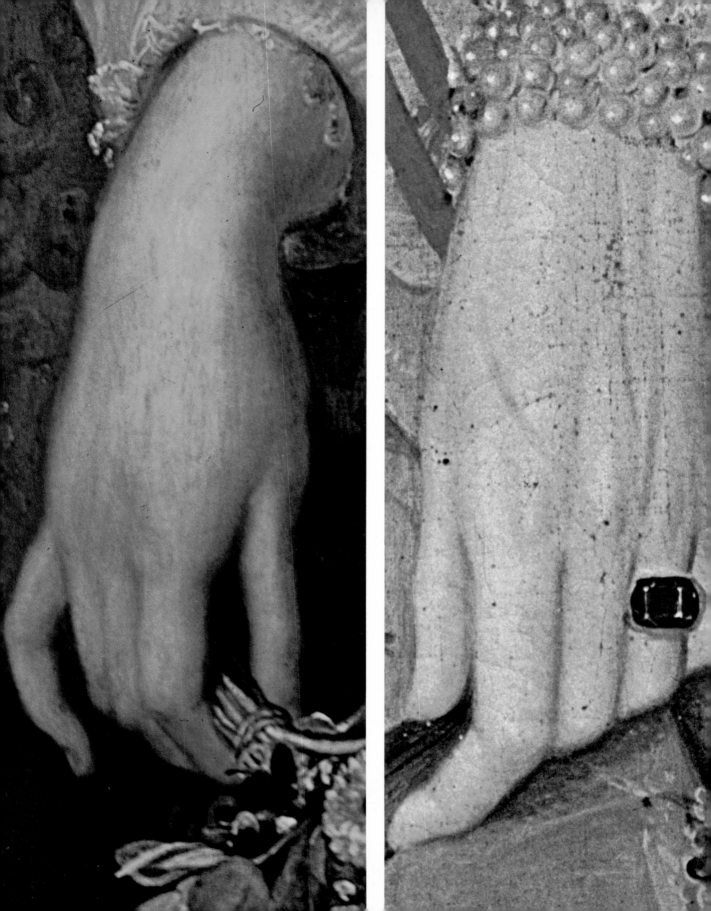

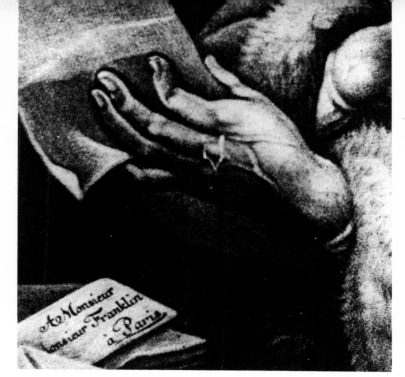

Left: the hands of Anne of Austria and of Elizabeth of England. Opposite: the hand of Benjamin Franklin. Below: the hand of the french writer Germaine de Staël.

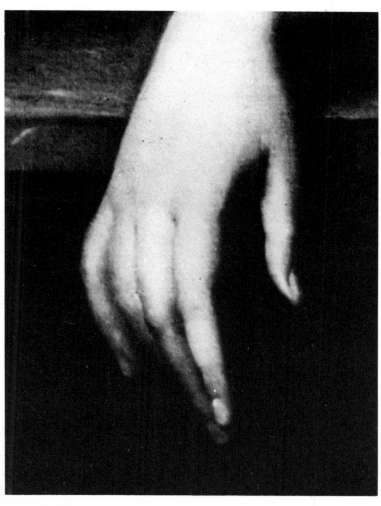

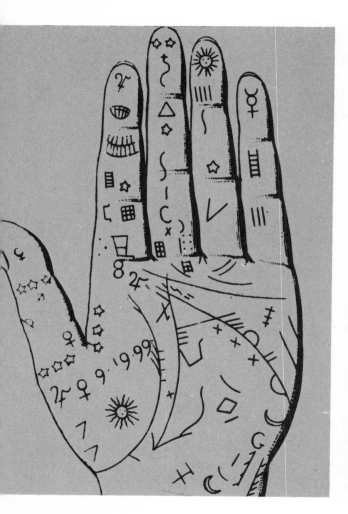

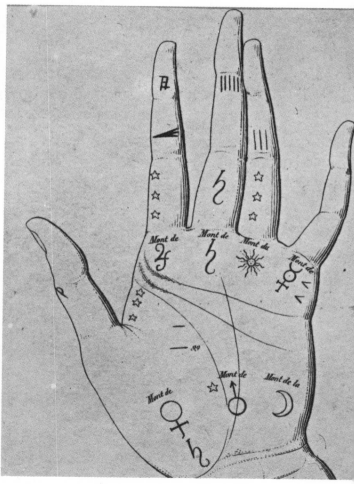

Famous hands: the hand of Napoleon. 2. The hand of Empress Josephine, his wife. One day, as she was finishing bathing in a stream in her native Martinique, an old Negress came up to her and read her palm, predicting that, eventually, she would become "more than a queen". 3. Right: the hand of Schiller. 4. A cast of the hands of Beethoven.

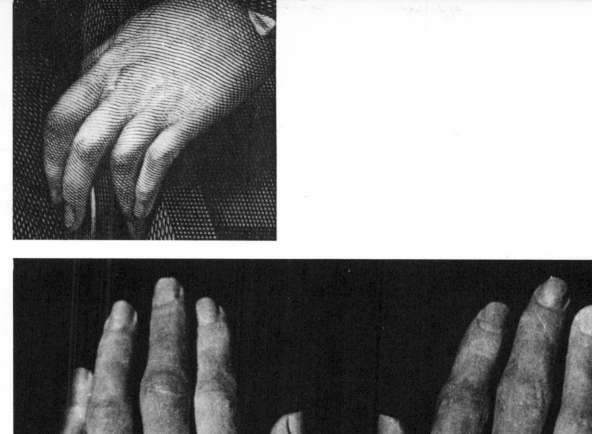
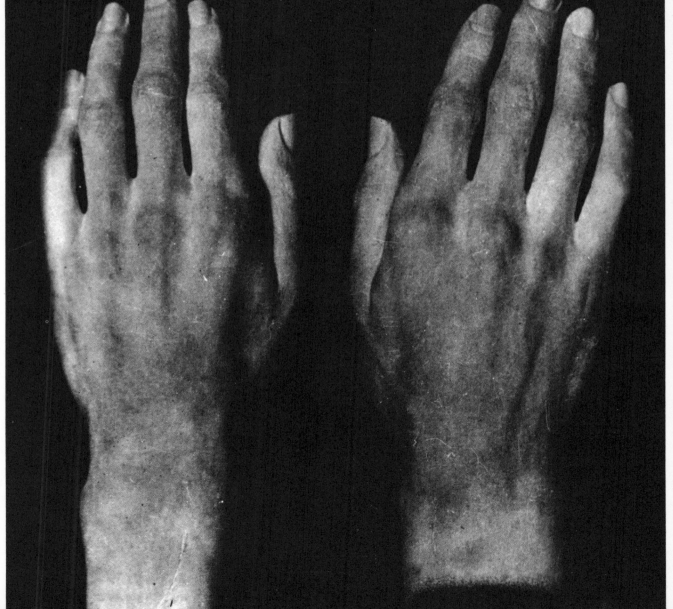

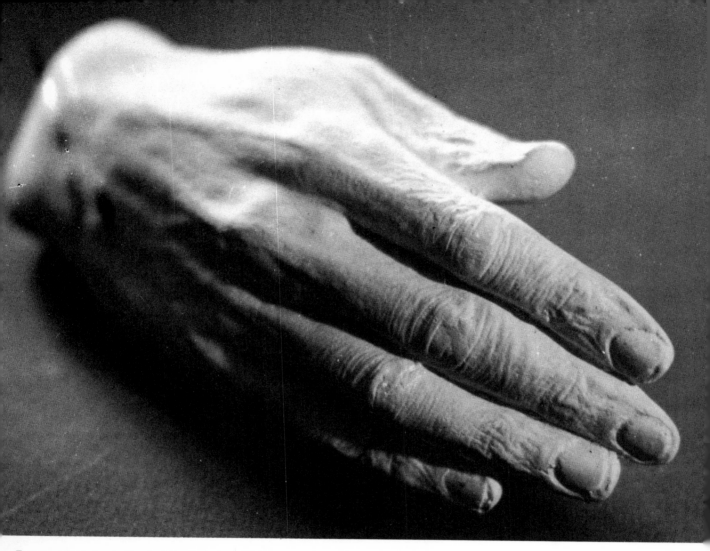

Famous hands: 1. Cast of the hand of Chopin. 2. The hands of virtuoso
pianist George Czifra. 3. Right: the hand of Balzac. Such pitiful lines . . .

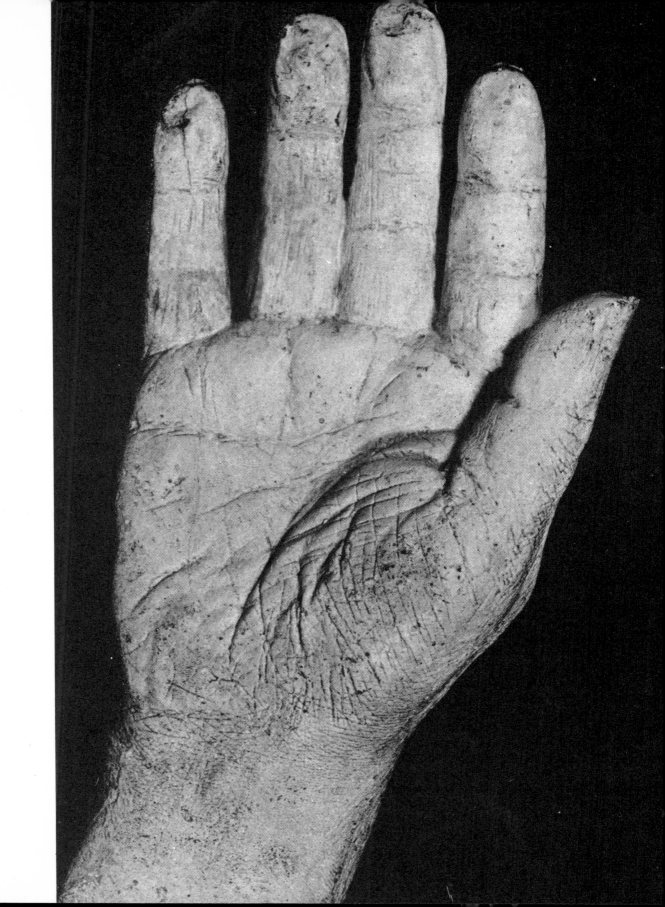

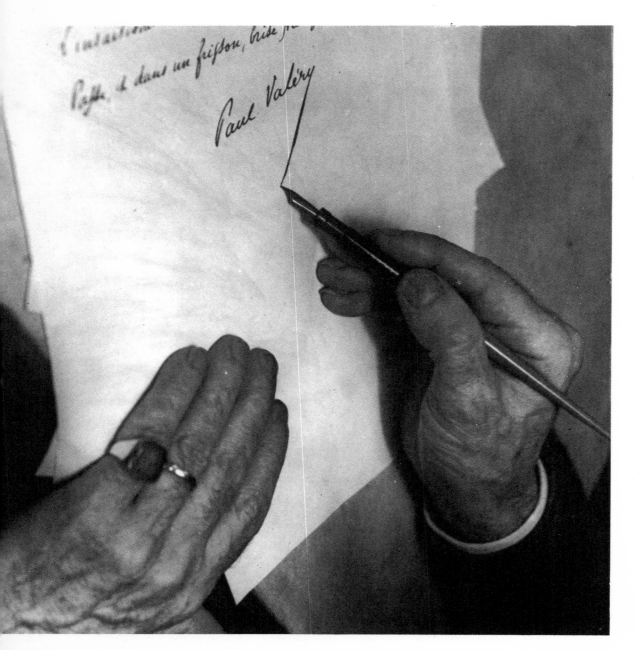

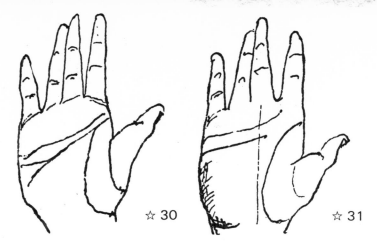

☆ 30   ☆ 31

line broken into chains, denotes swooning fits, weaknesses, and a generally lymphatic temperament.

☆ 30

If the Head Line is too close to the Heart Line, it suggests stifling, and occasional bouts of asthma; when forked, it means a fondness for dissimulation. If a number of small lines run across the Head Line, this is a sign of migraines.

☆ 31   When the Head Line begins at the same level as the Life Line, but apart from it, with a gap between, this is a sign of serious eye trouble in youth.

The Heart Line

If the Heart Line is long, though not so long as to cut right across the hand, and if it is distinct without being hollow, it denotes tenderness, kindness and loyal friendship. It may have a number of branches towards the percussion, below the Mount of Mercury (the *percussion* is so named because it is the striking edge of the palm) and it may send an offshoot towards Jupiter, which is evidence of heightened passion or

☆ 32   affection.

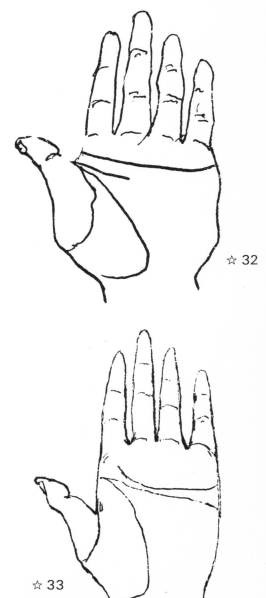

☆ 32

If it is hollow, straight and long enough to reach right across the hand, it denotes cruelty, malice and a propensity for violence, and even

☆ 33   for murder.

A Heart Line which runs very close to the Head Line often suggests hypocrisy, duplicity and cunning. If its point of departure is below the Mount of Saturn, one can expect to find a person with a poor capacity for warmth and affection. If the line breaks below Saturn, the hand of Fate will bring that life to a premature end.

If the Heart Line is made up of chains, it may denote inconstancy; its significance as far as health is concerned is more definite, however: it

☆ 33

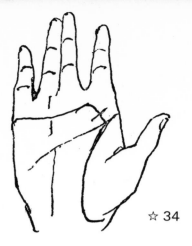

☆ 34

means that one is prone to heart disease or palpitations, or to anemia and a lymphatic state in general.

Besides a tendency towards wild passions, a red Heart Line may also suggest violence. Indeed, this trait has been found on the hands of many criminals.   ☆ 34

A pale Heart Line frequently denotes a cold, unfeeling debauchee. When the Heart Line slopes downwards, meeting the Head Line and the Life Line, and ends in a Cross of Saint Andrew on the Mount of Jupiter, it signifies a union or marriage which will bring with it losses or sufferings.   ☆ 35

When the Heart Line, *though not possessing such a sign,* joins with the Head Line and the Life Line, it is safe to predict a violent death, or a fatal accident. If the line occurs in both hands, it frequently denotes apoplexy.

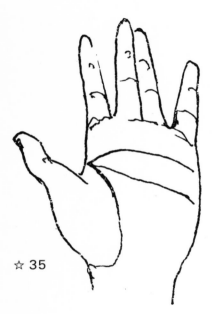

☆ 35

Dots on the Heart Line usually signify some a case of unrequited love: if the points occur below the Mount of Sun, the disappointment will stem from a passion for someone far above one's station in life. When a hand has no Heart Line at all, one may expect to find a lack of harmony in the organism as a whole, a lack of sensitivity towards the feelings of others, and, consequently, selfishness.   ☆ 36

If a Heart Line is a livid or dark yellowish color, it indicates, without any doubt, liver disease, this correlation having been established on the basis of observations made at Vichy, among people taking the waters there.

If the line is broken, particularly if the break occurs below Saturn, it is a sign of aneurism.

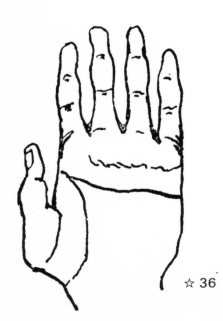

☆ 36

Below: in this hand, the Heart
Line seems to reveal a somewhat turbulent emotional life...

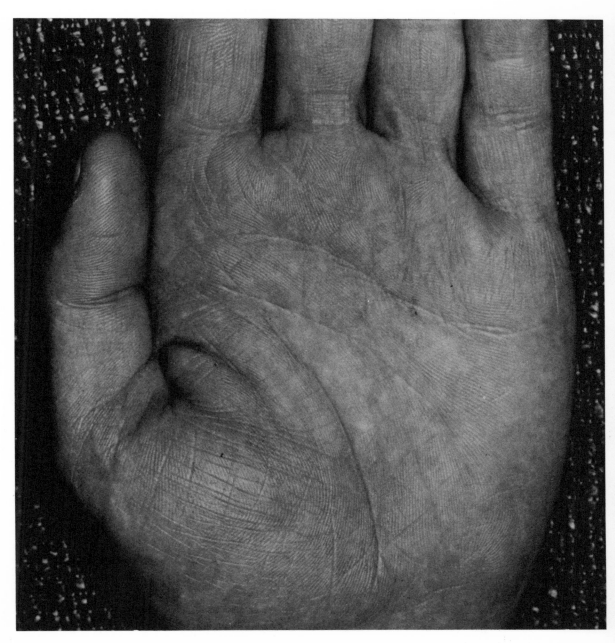

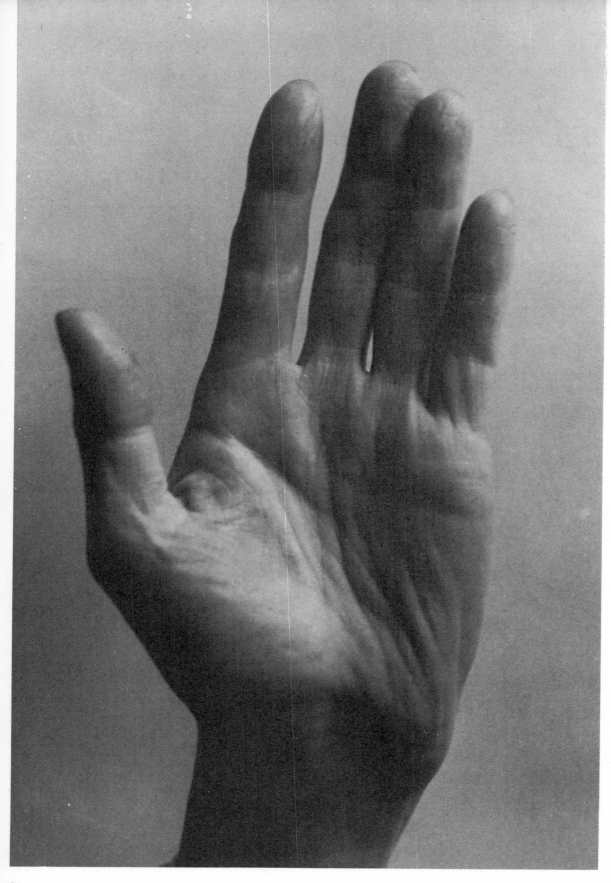

5. Other lines and signs

to 40 or 45. After leaving the Heart Line, it rises until its termination at the end of life. The curious thing about the Saturnine line is that one of the hands summarizes in a single line the whole of the events of a person's life, giving a total of good or bad fortune, whereas the other presents in detail the periods of difficulty or success, right up to the end of life, in the form of broken segments, the arrangement of which shows the ups and downs of Fate.

On the whole, the Fate Line begins to form at

Saturn, or the Line of Fate

The Line of Saturn, or Fate Line, should ideally begin at the rascette line, and climb to the Mount of Saturn; such a line, if it is straight, well-traced ☆ 37 and uninterrupted, is the best of its kind.

Saturn is the *fatum* of the ancient world, the line which announces one's destiny. It is the counterpart of the events registered on the Life Line. It states the same facts, but gives less detail about them, especially where timing is concerned, because it is not measured in degrees, as the Life Line is. Moreover, there is no reason why it should be, because, generally speaking, the paths of these two lines correspond, so that the Life Line explains the events which appear on the Line of Saturn only in the form of a cross, a star, a black dot or a break.

It should be consulted from the bottom up. From the rascette line to the Head Line it represents about thirty years; it is therefore easy to place certain events in time, on that basis. This line reproduces, one might almost say reflects, the major events of Fate, even of the favorable kind, though it usually adds some subtle distinction which broadens the area for divination. The section which runs from the Head Line to the Heart Line, marks the period from the age of 30

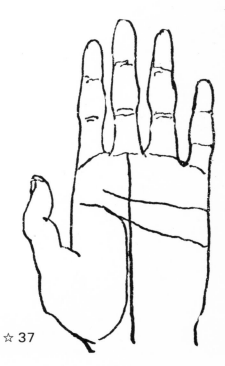

☆ 37

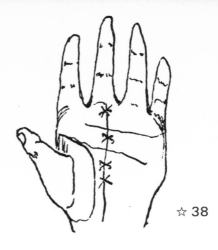

☆ 38

the moment when a favorable position has taken shape, even when the true state of good fortune arrives later; note, however, that it forms a deeper groove as soon as it becomes assured. ☆ 38

Changes of worldly position are indicated by a cross, and it is possible to see whether these changes have been favorable or otherwise. A star in the middle of the Fate Line always denotes misfortune, whether past or future. It has frequently happened that reversals of fortune have thus been predicted during a highly satisfactory period, and have invariably come to pass, sometimes only a month after the prediction itself.

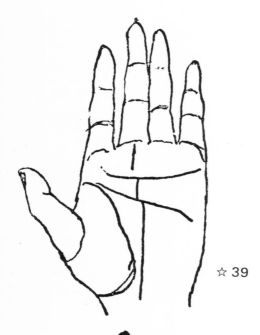

☆ 39

The Fate Line frequently stops near the Head Line; in a very large number of cases, it stops very suddenly after a beautifully traced, quite brilliant section, and either disappears completely or re-appears five, ten or fifteen years later, only to break off again and emerge some short while further on. The combinations of the Fate and Life Lines provide some exceedingly strange explanations; vast amounts of fine detail are often given also, as the reader will see in the many illustrated examples in this book. ☆ 39

The Fate Line is also the place to look for signs of adultery, and the duration of each affair. Adultery, for either sex, is often related to, or accounts for, a loss of worldly position; while, in other cases, it may mean the acquisition of a brilliant fortune. The duration of a case of adultery is indicated by the length of the sign—an island—which is illustrated here. There are some islands which cause the whole hand to be subject to the influence of the Fate Line, and sometimes to that of the Sun Line; this latter type promise a brilliant future, particularly when the thumb, as seen in the illustration, is long enough to signify a dominant will, and is accompanied by ☆ 40

☆ 40

a long Head Line, which denotes the acquisitive impulse: the kind of will-power which, being backed up by powerful reason, is all the more formidable. As can be seen from the illustration, these lines, when very long, are a sign of a union which will last a whole life-time, or a great part thereof, depending on their size. It need not mean marriage; a union contracted with a person who has been living for a long time with someone else is all that is needed for this island to become formed. Accordingly, a man separated from his wife, or a woman separated from her husband, bear this sign if they get involved with someone else. Some islands have branches which meet at the end of life and confer a regular status upon this union.

A very intense love for someone of the opposite sex who is either married or deeply involved with someone else may be a sufficient cause for the appearance of this island, even if the loved one is unaware of the other's feelings. This island may occur in the hand of a married person who loves in silence; if the object of such a passion is distinguished, either by talent, worldly position or wealth, the person experiencing such emotions will have a star attached to an inclined ☆ 41 cross on the Mount of Jupiter.

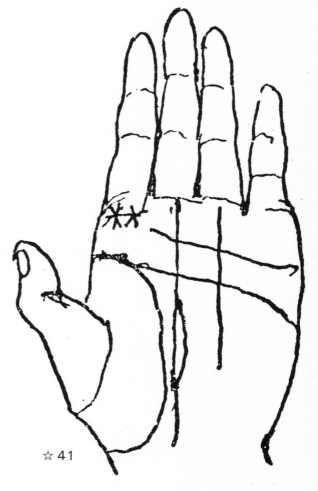

☆ 41

Some people have no Fate Line at all; accordingly, they have neither good fortune nor bad fortune, and no major obstacles to overcome. They may also never be particularly lucky, but, usually, they are fairly insensitive people, who manage to make the best of whatever comes their way. Their hands are certainly not hands of ill-fortune, which usually belong to people for whom peace and quiet is the principal happiness. The Fate Line is a mark of sensitivity. Those who are engaged in painful or heavy work do not have this line; as proved by plaster-casts taken during scientific expeditions, Eskimos do not

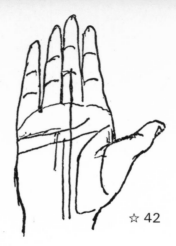

☆ 42

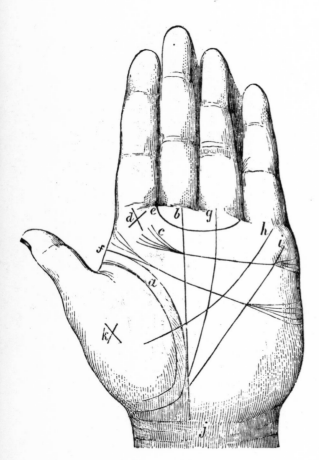

Picture of a happy hand: a) double line of life.
b) absolute happiness (direct line of Saturn).
c) one line is all that is needed. d) a union of
love. e) Girdle of Venus. f) complete genius,
order, administration, clarity (only one line
needed). g) success in the arts, renown, wealth.
h) union of Mercury and Venus, perspicacity in
business, love and fortune. The line should
begin from the Life Line, and not from within
the mount. i) a sound temperament, and a perfect
stomach. j) triple magic bracelet, long life.
k) a single love.

have a Fate Line. And this is only to be expected:
if the harsh conditions under which they live
made much of an impression on them, they
would probably lose the will to live.

The Fate Line is, in a sense, a mark of distinction in creation. Hyper-sensitive types have
a very irregular Fate Line, with a heavily lined
hand, and are therefore in a constant state of irritability. A break occurring in the Fate Line at the
junction with the Head Line is a misfortune
caused by a miscalculation.

If it stops at the Heart Line, it refers to a misfortune attributable to love or parental inter-
ference, and, quite often, to a change of destiny
following upon a separation or a divorce.   ☆ 42

If the Fate Line enters the third phalange of the
finger, reaching as far as the second joint, it is a
fatalistic sign which sometimes even means a
spell behind bars. If it is intersected, on the
Mount of Saturn, by a great number of cross-
lines, it means that obstacles will be encountered in every field of activity; if the sign
takes the form of the rungs of a ladder, it is quite
likely that prison may be involved, and quite certain that there will be a succession of misfortunes. A square formed by these same lines
on the mount itself means protection against
disaster, as we have already seen.

A simple, straight, well-traced Fate Line on the
Mount of Saturn denotes happiness and good
health in old age, as Saturn is the emblem of old
age in chiromancy. Saturnine types usually live
to a ripe old age, and old people gradually as-
sume the signatures of Saturn.

If the Fate Line swings towards Jupiter and
stops on the Mount of that name, it is a sign of
good fortune, particularly for scholars, scientists
and the like, and means that their works will
bring them fame and fortune.

The nails can be a very revealing subject for
study. Above: the nails of a Chinese scholar.

☆ 43

Sun Line

The Sun Line is somewhat complicated; it is a less abundant source of indications than the Fate Line. It represents calm composure, talent, ☆ 43 modesty and the kind of self-esteem that needs no outward displays to sustain itself. It is a sign of fame, wealth, love of art, distinctions won by one's own merits. If this line is straight, hollow, well traced and unmarked, it means great wealth when the hand is dominated by the Mounts of Jupiter or Mercury and when its relief is, in general, more subdued. A well developed Mount of Sun which does *not* have a line confers on its owner a taste for the beautiful, the noble and the simple, but does not mean that he will actually produce any works which embody those qualities. The Sun Line indicates a man who puts his aptitudes into practical artistic effect, thereby becoming famous.

If there are several Sun Lines, the individual is able to devote himself to a number of different arts at the same time and make a success of them all; however, one single line is more likely to succeed. If two or three such lines, all equally well traced, straight and distinct, occur on the mount, they might indicate a superior man who is both famous, rich and prominent in society. Lamartine had three Sun Lines, but two of them were broken. The Sun Line is to be found in the hands of all those who occupy important positions or possess great wealth.

Artists, scientists, writers and the élite of the medical profession always have Sun Lines of varying length and quality.

Cross-lines on this line mean difficulties, struggles, financial loss; this is particularly so if these lines occur in both hands. When they occur in one hand only, they mean that success will be

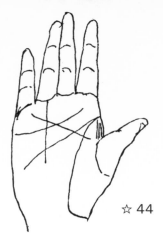

☆ 44

☆ 44 achieved only after immense effort.

If several Sun Lines are tortuous and unevenly distributed on the mount they mean that the individual tends to dabble in a number of different branches of art, spreading his talents so thin that he rarely achieves noteworthy results in any of them. When the point of departure of the line is a small island, low on the Mount of Sun, an adultery has helped the person in question reach the top. When the point of departure is on the Moon (caprices) and the line goes straight up the Mount of Sun, it means that worldly success has been the result of protection received from some powerful quarter. When the line rises, but is crossed by streaks which do not cut deeply across it, ambition will be thwarted by envy or perhaps also by malice on the part of the person's superiors.

In any case, a well traced Sun Line is one of the most favorable signs a person can have, partic-
☆ 45 ularly if he or she is an artist.

The Sun Line, which represents clarity, should always be consulted in chiromantic practice as a definitive proof. The Fate Line may be superb, but if the Sun Line is lacking, and, above all, if it is lacking between the Head and Heart Lines, one may safely that the person's destiny will be upset by a number of adverse incidents. If the Sun Line, while running parallel to the Fate Line through this area, which is known as the *quadrangle,* breaks up into several sections, the obstacles encountered in the individual's destiny will be even more formidable; his destiny, while not completely ruined, will brought to a halt in
☆ 46 successive periods.

If the Sun Line contains a star or a grouping of random lines, a catastrophe will occur, though if the line continues it means some event which is often followed by success. If these lines occur inside the quadrangle, which can be divided into

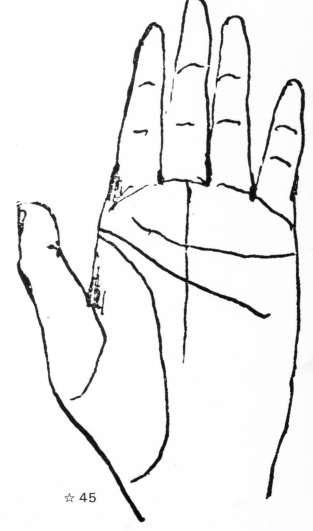

☆ 45

about ten years, a disaster will happen which, while not actually destroying the individual's happiness altogether, may well jeopardize his position or his reputation, of whatever sort it may be, since these are traits specially represented by the Sun. Moreover, *any sign in this space, however, insignificant it may seem,* is worthy of close scrutiny, for the Sun Line rarely begins lower down the hand; nonetheless, the obstacle will be directly proportional to the size of the sign, and may, on occasion, indicate nothing more than an emotional upset.

Cross-lines, indicating the upheavals or misfortunes in a person's life, very often explain the cause of an adversity shown in the Sun Line or in the form of a broken Fate Line, and they do this while at the same time describing much more precisely the period at which the calamity in question will occur. The observer should therefore take careful note of the indications given by the cross-lines originating on the Mount of Venus, and should, at the same time, look for the corresponding stigmata in the Sun Line and the Fate Line. In this way, he will arrive at some astonishing results which will have been verified twice.

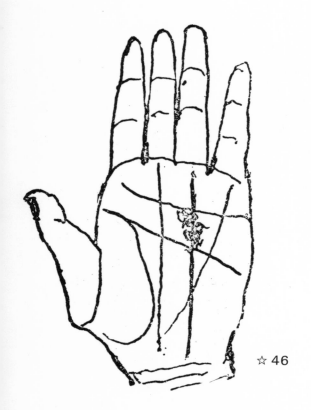

☆ 46

Hepatic line or Liver line
☆ 47

This line originates on the rascette line, near the Life Line; its importance lies in the fact that, when it is well traced, it denotes a good stomach; in fact, superb specimens of this line have been found in quite old people, even though their Life Line was none too impressive.

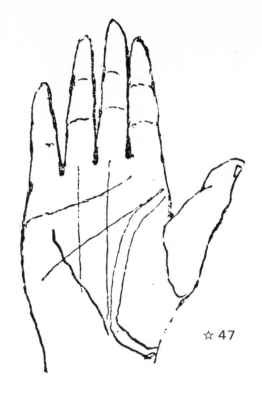

☆ 47

When the hepatic line is missing from a hand, it often means great physical agility; it also means a tight, closed skin which does not sweat readily and consequently makes its owner more prone to headaches and migraines.

If the hepatic line forms a triangle with the Head Line, it denotes a capacity for the occult sciences.

A hepatic line which is strongly colored indicates brutality and arrogance; while if it is tortuous and contains a variety of colors, it may signify liver disease, most particularly if the lines are black and yellow. In fact, this one type of coloring is the most unmistakable sign of this kind of disease.

The Girdle of Venus ☆ 48

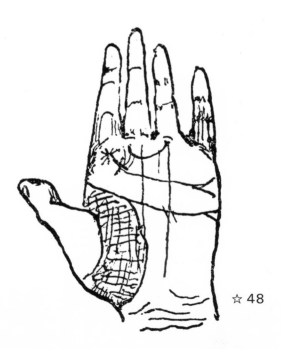

☆ 48

As the illustration shows, the Girdle of Venus begins between the Mount of Jupiter and the Mount of Saturn, slopes gently downwards, follows a semi-circular course and terminates in the palmar area between the third and fourth fingers. Those who have a Girdle of Venus, a lined Mount of Venus and a long Head Line—meaning self-control—are capable of exercising enormous attractive power over the objects of their lust; while true of both sexes, this applies particularly to women. A mature, sensible person—especially a Sun-type with a long Head Line—can combat this kind of sensual attraction, thereby acquiring psychic energy which will confer upon him or her authentic moral superiority.
☆ 49

The photo on the right was taken in Tokyo. A chiromantist's stall.

Stars

A star heralds an event which seems beyond the control of our free will, even though its effects can be successfully resisted by the force of reason and will-power. It is usually situated on the mounts of the palm and on the lines; occasionally a star can be seen in other parts of the hand, indicating illnesses and their relative gravity: wherever they appear, stars have a meaning, which may, occasionally, be quite favorable.

☆ 50

On the Mount of Jupiter, a star is always favorable, meaning satisfied ambition, honors, happiness in love, a sudden rise in the world, and predestination for great things. A star on the Mount of Jupiter, connected to a cross of union, always leads to love or marriage with a person whose social standing is higher than one's own.

This is an infallible sign. The illustration shows the signs which may explain personal magnetism and nervous fascination: an ambitious, Jupiter-type hand, both sensual and clever, sometimes even a rounded thumb: unrelenting perseverance. But a star accompanied by a cross of union may also be found in the hand of a highly meritorious and talented person.

A star on the first phalange of the middle finger (Saturn) indicates events beyond the normal human powers of prediction, a glorious career such as that of Napoleon, for example; however, if the organism is not equal to the challenge presented to it by destiny, it can mean madness.

A star on the Mount of Saturn is always a threatening sign, heralding paralysis, an untimely death and a disease which is quite likely to be incurable. When this sign is very pronounced, it may also indicate a murder.

☆ 51

A star on the Mount of Mercury is a sign of

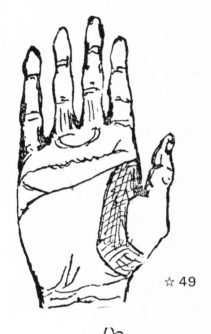

☆ 49

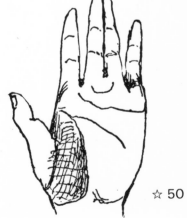

☆ 50

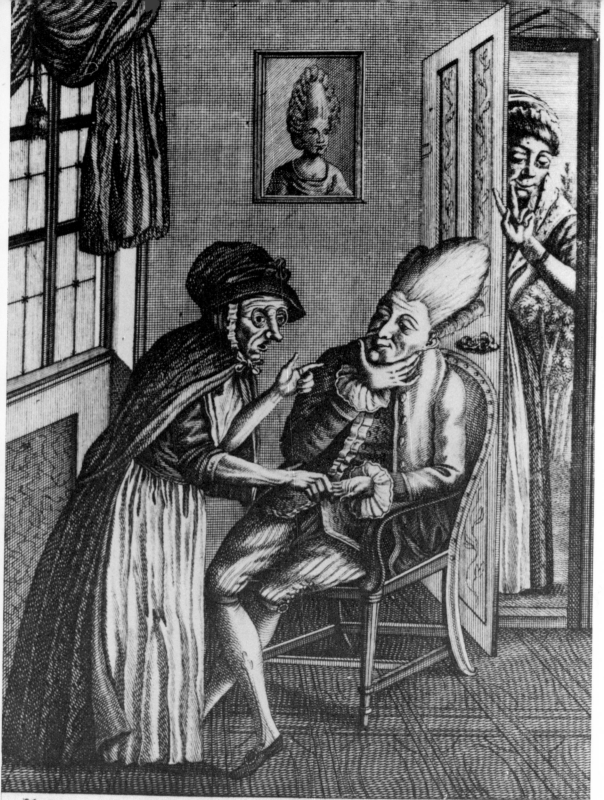

Verändern Sie einst Ihren Stand,
so seh ich aus der flachen Hand,
daß sich auf Ihrer Liebsten Treu
vollkommen zuverlaßen sey.

Monsieur! si vous changés l'etat
Je vous prognostique par la main,
Que l'on a beau à se fier
Sur le coeur sincere de la votre.

Opposite: 16th-century engraving; below: British print, 18th century (after Reynolds). Right: German engraving, 18th century.

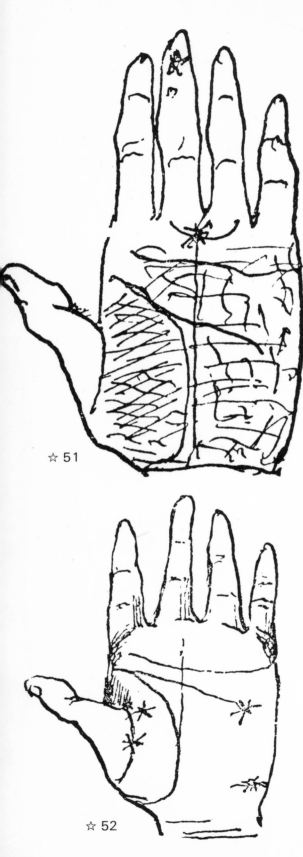

☆ 51

☆ 52

theft and crooked dealings in general, particularly if the person's hand already has various other adverse chiromantic features.

☆ 52

A star on the Mount of Moon represents an illness involving water, such as hydropsy; it also indicates disorders of the bladder, and, most frequently, death by drowning or great danger in a shipwreck, especially if it lies on a Travel Line on the percussion near the Moon.

A star placed across the lower part of the second phalange of the thumb, above the line which separates that phalange from the mount, means unhappiness caused by women, and preeminently a disastrous marriage, most often where Saturn- and Sun-types are concerned. Jupiter-types are the only ones capable of resisting this influence; and even they are often helped by the sudden death of their spouse, especially at a critical moment, such as the concluding stages of an unsuccessful and disastrously costly law-suit. The star may occur on the line itself.

The star at the bottom of the Head Line denotes madness or a head injury. A star on the Mount of Venus is a sign of the death of parents or friends.

The square

The square may be formed by several normally formed lines in the middle of the palm, though it does quite often occur without the help of lines at all. In either case, it denotes preservation from danger or adversity.

☆ 53

This writer remembers a particularly striking case of such a feature occurring on the hand of a house painter who had fallen three times from the scaffolding around a building: once from the sixth floor, then from the third and later from the

fourth floor, and escaping with nothing more than shock and bruises, without breaking a single bone. In such an incident, the man in question had fallen into a huge vat which a jam-manufacturer happened to have left outside in the yard to cool!

This same sign has been noted in people who succeeded in eluding would-be murderers and in many other similar cases. The square in the painter's hand was situated on the finger of Saturn, at precisely the spot where the star of murder occurs. There can be no doubt that a star framed by a square on the Mount of Saturn means an attempted murder which proves unsuccessful.

Dots

A dot denotes a serious injury if it is deep, and a nervous disorder if it is blackish or bluish. In the lines, a light blue is the most alarming color. It means nervous disorders, rather than madness. Madness is indicated by a star.

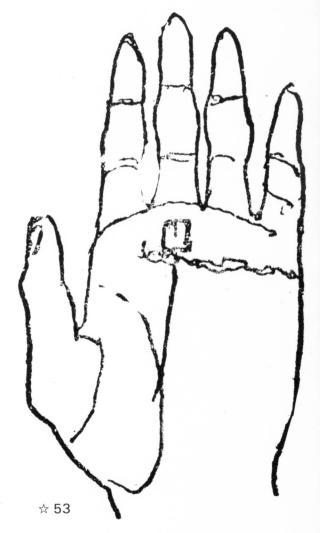

☆ 53

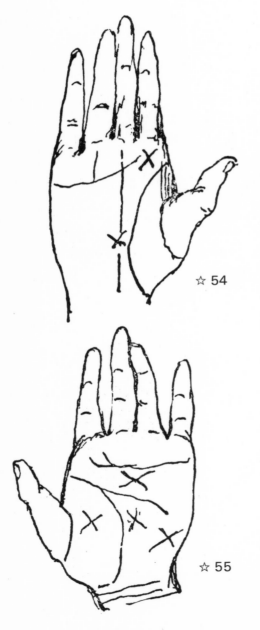

☆ 54

☆ 55

Crosses   ☆ 54

Crosses represent changes in worldly position, when a line of Fate, for example, is broken and resumes with a cross. Saint Andrew's cross, X, on the Mount of Jupiter, means marriage or an affair of the heart; we have already noted the fortunate significance of these crosses when they are accompanied by a star.

A cross denoting an affair or marriage often occurs in the hands of both partners, even though the love between them is not equally shared; this is quite a common phenomenon, particularly in the hands of very pretty women. It is assumed, wrongly perhaps, that pretty women rarely respond with equal enthusiasm to the passionate advances which come their way. In such circumstances, one may conclude that one has been married out of sheer love. This is certainly the case when the Fate Line or the Sun Line originates on the Mount of Moon, meaning caprice, passionate attachments and advancement in the world due to powerful patronage.

Even though crosses on the Mount of Jupiter are usually a good sign, when they are connected to a star, they also can have a much less favorable connotation: a cross on Mercury is a bad sign which strongly suggests that one's integrity is a fault.   ☆ 55

A cross in the area known as the quadrangle denotes a capacity for mysticism. A cross in the middle of the Plain of Mars (the hollow of the palm below the Head Line) is a sign of a quarrelsome man.

A large cross on the Mount of Moon: exalted notions, a tendency to exaggerate, in both words and ideas.

A cross on the Mount of Venus means one single, consuming love.

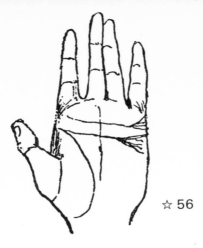

☆ 56

☆ 56 Branches

Ascending, continuous branches are always a favorable sign. Some writers have claimed that branches situated at the beginning or end of the Head and Heart Lines are good omens. Yet it should be noted that those occurring *at the end* of the Head Line may also mean a loss of brain power.

☆ 57

Those who have a heavily lined Mount of Moon have an advanced prophetic sense, most especially if the Mounts of Moon and Mercury are joined by an arched line.

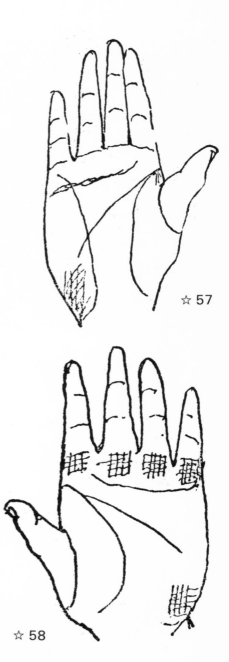

☆ 57

Grilles (Grids)

☆ 58

As chiromantic symbols, grilles represent obstacles, relating in each case to the qualities proper to each mount. Grilles on Jupiter mean that the qualities or favorable opportunities offered by that mount are impeded in some way; on Saturn, they mean a great misfortune or even imprisonment; on the Mount of Sun, they represent impotence or mean that solar inspiration has lost its impetus; and on Mercury they signify a propensity for theft, devious behavior or the misuse of science.

Grilles on the Moon mean soaring imagination, anxiety, nervous spasms, and, if a star occurs simultaneously on Saturn, a tendency towards hemiplegia; however, when the hand also contains a finely traced Sun Line, the individual will be fond of poetry and literature, and have a lyrical frame of mind generally. These grilles also indicate poor functioning of the kidneys.

People who have grilles on the Mount of Moon, especially when the whole of the hand is densely lined, are forever moving about restlessly, while everything around them is calm; in

☆ 58

Left: ''the lines of the hand'', by Gro-
maire. (Paris, Musée d'Art Moderne).
Below: in Thaïland.

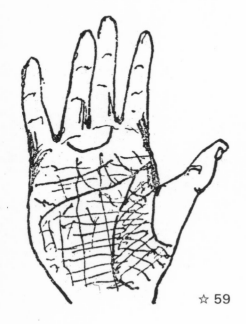

☆ 59

this they resemble the poplar and the aspen, whose leaves seem to be constantly in motion, even when the wind has died down and left the rest of the trees in the forest quite motionless. A Girdle of Venus makes such people even more sensitive.

☆ 59

Grilles on the Mount of Venus give one a taste for exotic, and often lascivious pleasures; if the Sun Line is good and the Head Line is straight, in a hand with a strong thumb, the grilles on the Mount of Venus can stimulate one's nervous energy and, consequently one's imagination, to the point where a great upsurge in creative intensity occurs. At certain times, grilles may mean additional strength, except for those occurring on Jupiter and Saturn, which remain adverse.

Stripes

When there are a large number of stripes on a single mount or finger, they denote electric energy, of the quality associated with that mount or finger. These are the outermost manifestations of a deeper life-force, just as the surface ripples of a gushing mountain stream suggest the tumultuous energy beneath. In order to be favorable, however, these stripes should always be ascending, as stripes lying across the finger represent obstacles to the exercise of the particular ability or function associated with that finger. The degree of aptitude varies according to the number of stripes present on the finger, just as very thick smoke is a distant signal of a very intense fire. A heavily striped finger of Mercury (little finger) denotes a person especially active in one of the many pursuits related to Mercury, and often gifted in all of them, but most particularly in medicine. The same is true of the finger of the Sun (third or ring finger). Saturn will in-

☆ 60

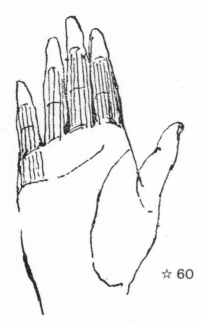

☆ 60

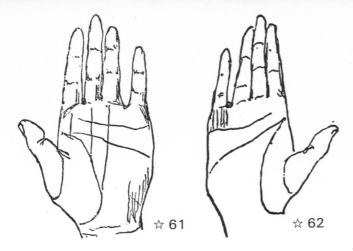

☆ 61 ☆ 62

dicate a special aptitude for mining or prospecting, botany, chemistry or agriculture. Jupiter will be more likely to impart abilities connected with careers in administration or diplomacy.

Stripes ascending from the Life Line are always favorable and often indicate strokes of good fortune emanating *from one's own personal merits.* On the mounts, these stripes, with the exception of the mounts situated below the fingers, suggest a high degree of irritability; this is most true of the Mount of Mars which, when deeply lined, almost always represents violence, on the moral plane, and bronchitis or disorders of the larynx. Vertical stripes on the Moon often mean diarrhea. If placed vertically above the

☆ 61

Head Line, but without intersecting that line, these stripes, if they are present in small numbers, may denote the triumph of intelligent ideas; the same kind of stripes on the Heart Line serve no useful purpose and can be positively harmful. In any case, they rarely occur in that position.   ☆ 62

On the Mount of Mercury, deeply traced, numerous or tightly packed stripes are a sign of an aptitude for science. People who bear this kind of stigmata—whether they be in the arts, sciences, literature or business—either derive great pleasure from reading medical books or they have developed their own instinctive brand of medicine, which they practise on themselves and

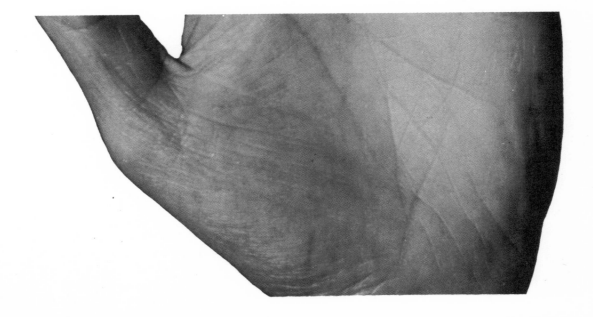

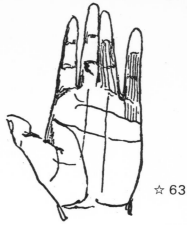

☆ 63

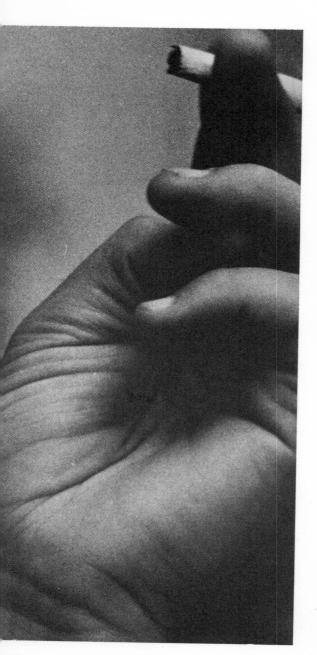

on their friends. Such people had intended at one time or another to devote themselves to medicine entirely, but were obliged, by events beyond their control, to go into other careers.

It is unusual for all the fingers of a hand to be striped. If that were to happen it would be difficult to distinguish the main aptitude from the rest. But the fingers of Mercury and Sun, in the case of scholars, scientists and artists, are often both striped at the same time. The first phalange, which bears the nail, and the sense of touch, rarely has many such lines.   ☆ 63

Lines on the Mount of Mars are harmful, as we have seen. A well-developed Mount of Mars with no lines gives a spirit of resignation, particularly when the Mount of Moon is full and smooth. It is the Mount of Moon, with supporting signs from the Mount of Mars, which indicates the most fearless seafarers, most expecially when the hand as a whole is hard.

The rascette line

The rascette is a line traced along the joint of the wrist. It forms a kind of bracelet, and is often double or triple.

In chiromancy, these lines each signify between twenty-five and thirty years of life. Three superb and well-traced lines form what the chiromantists of ancient times used to call the *magic bracelet*—that is, health and wealth. Today, less importance is attached to the perfection of this sign, though it is still a very good omen, particularly if the hand is otherwise characterized by intelligence and energy. The ancients believed that a cross in the middle of the rascette lines meant an inheritance; in fact, it meant as many inheritances as there were crosses.

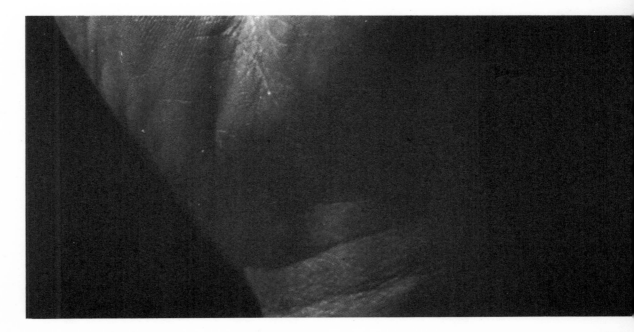

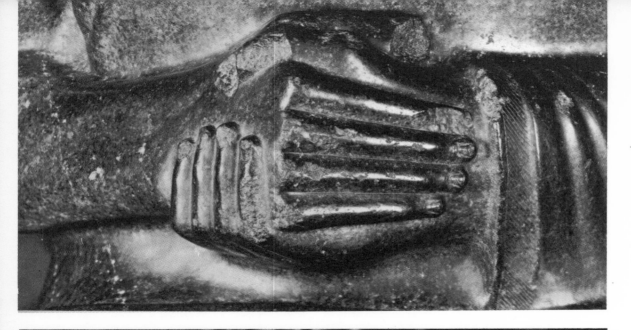

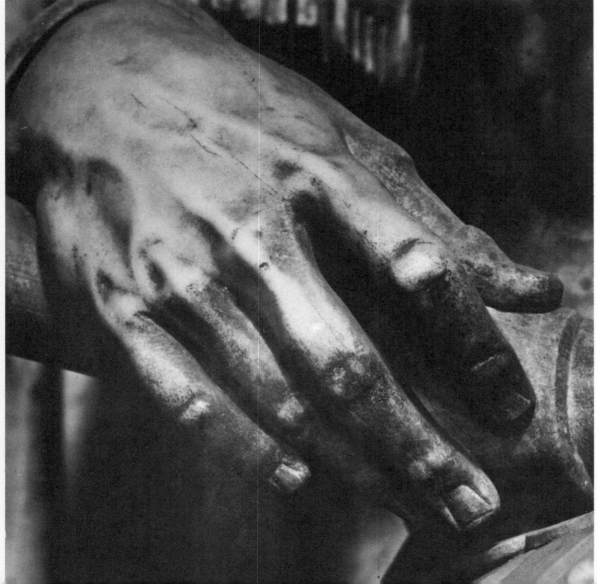

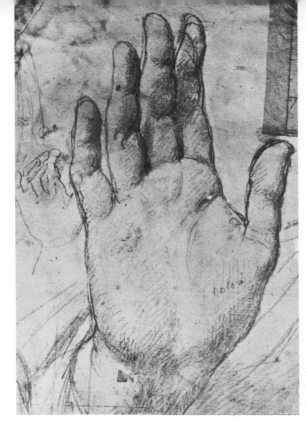

Hands in art: the architect of Gudea (Assyrian art); the hand of Julian de Medicis (Florence); studies of the hand, by Ingres; the "hand of God", by Rodin; (Picasso).

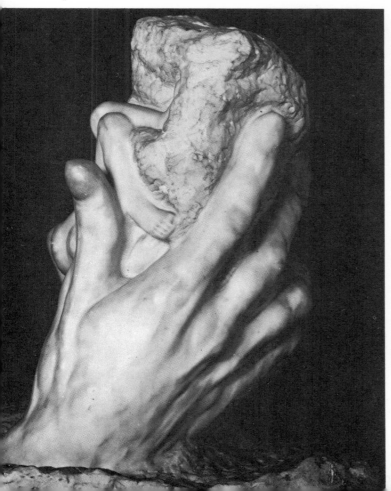

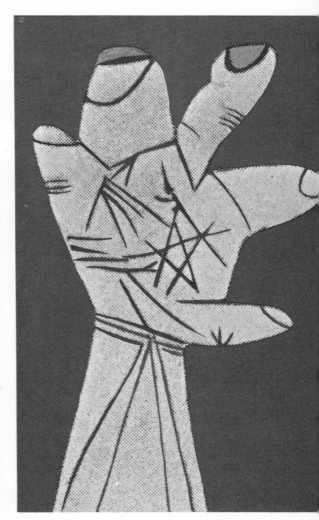

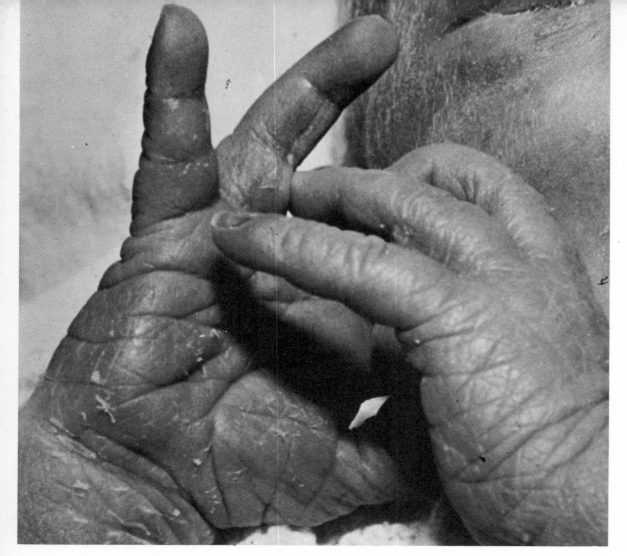

Who thought that the lines of the hand were caused by the act of folding or closing it? A point of crucial importance is that these lines exist from the moment of birth *(see photo, above)*. Moreover, the hand of a baby can be remarkably expressive *(see photo, opposite)*.

Right hand page: two types of women—and hands. The lower picture shows a person who is clearly overwhelmed by the sufferings of life; nevertheless, this is a truly noble hand.

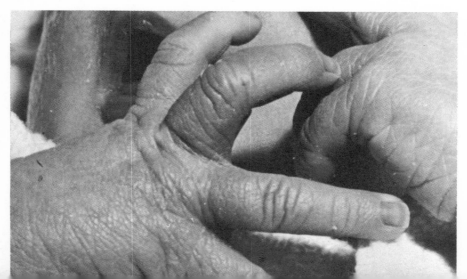

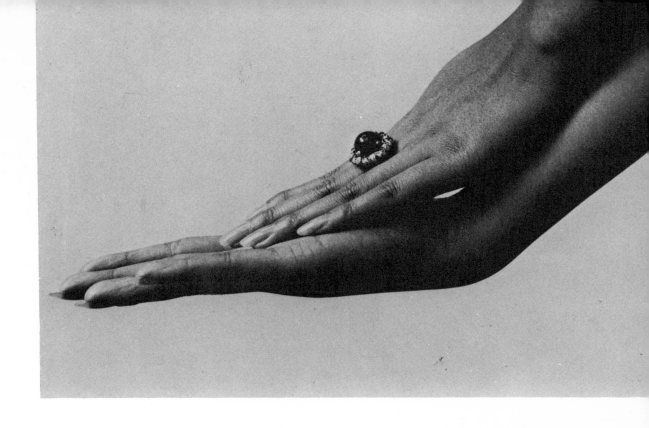

Psycho-Physiology of the Hand

Some readers will find this text easier to assimilate than others; yet all will agree that it confirms, if confirmation were necessary, the extremely serious nature of the study of the hand, in all its aspects.

The hand is far more than the mere dictionary definition, that is, the part of the human body situated at the end of the arm and used for grasping and touching: it is the organ of our concrete contacts with the real world. Man has sometimes been defined as the only animal having two upper extremities, two hands. Since then, however, Darwinist and neo-Darwinist theories have pointed out the falsehood of this definition; the anatomical and embryological comparison of the upper extremities of quadrumanes with those of man has shown that, in the higher forms of ape, the toe of the upper extremities has a special kind of mobility: rather than a mere foot, it is "prehensile" extremity.

Civilization and the psychological use of the hand have accentuated the greater, more radical difference between the lower and upper extremities. Our objective rendering of our spatial intuitions and our sensations derives from the first, uncertain contact of our ancestors' hands with the world around them, a contact which was to become bolder and more sophisticated with the passage of time.

The anatomical differences between the foot and the hand really amount to the following: the small bones of the tarsus, which is similar to the carpus of the hand, are arranged in quite a different pattern; some muscles, common to both organs, are used in different ways, while others are found in one but not in the other—the long peroneal, for example, the muscle which gives mobility and solidity to the big toe, is not found in the hand. A further, and rather minor point is that the hand muscles corresponding to the short flexor and short extensor muscles of the toes are rather long. This accounts for the greater and more varied mobility of the fingers, when compared with the toes.

Of all the muscles of the hand, the most "psychic", that is, the muscle which is most closely involved in the psychic functions, is the long flexor of the thumb, followed by all the other flexor muscles of the fingers. In cases of writer's cramp, nervous cramp and infectious or other forms of paralysis, it is interesting to note that the flexors are most severely affected. Apart from purely psychological considerations and the changes inherent in toxic processes, this may well be due to some special disposition of the original neurons. In apes, the thumb is not flexed by an independent muscle.

Besides being an anatomical feature of man, the hand is therefore also a psychological feature, on account of its extraordinary mobility, the many uses to which it is put, and the major role it plays in social psychology.

There are depressed hands, just as there are gay hands, agile hands, nervous hands and sad hands. Certain hands are tender and voluptuous, others are lazy, while yet others are full of energy. The most beautiful hand that I have ever seen conveyed to me an impression of the most total harmony. The fingers of certain types of neurotic subjects reach a stage where they are no longer really independently mobile; their movement is limited, and fixed, just like the gestures of a man whose brain has been damaged.

One of the first features of the hand that should be examined is the skin, as it provides the chiromantist with a remarkable source of precise information. For example, the finger-tips are an extremely sensitive area, equipped with an abundance of tactile corpuscles; because of their specific structure and their high concentration of blood vessels their tactile sensitivity ranks very high, second only to that of the lips and the area around the eyes.

The palm of the hand is richer than the back of the hand; amongst other reasons this is so because of the median nerve. Besides the nerve endings, the palm has a number of tiny swellings, or tactile corpuscles; these are more numerous between the interdigital spaces, where the swellings of the skin are located. Sometimes, there are as many as three hundred of them in the palm of one hand, in the area next to the fingers, near an interdigital space.

For some scientists, the hand is the supreme organ of touch, while for others it is the essential organ of feeling. Both definitions are true and mutually complementary. In blind people and certain others who have developed their tactile sensitivity, this faculty reaches an extraordinary degree of refinement. It maintains a constant relationship with the distribution of the tactile corpuscles, and is duller in the palm than on the edges and back of the hand.

The coloring and delicacy of the skin are highly significant psycho-physiological indicators. The feel of the skin readily gives one an idea of a person's occupation, and of his degree of sensitivity.

The lines of the hand change; yet, although their exact topography is not fixed, the observer may draw guidance from their general form and particularly from their physiognomy. The "Life Line" merely demarcates the muscles of the area of the thumb; similarly, the "Heart Line" is a fold formed mechanically by the knuckles. The fact that these lines are dictated by real, dynamic needs therefore emphasizes their fundamental role in the study of the psychology of the hand.

The "Head Line", however, is much less precise; it is a shallower fold in the skin of the palm, and is not attributable to an articulation or to any specific muscular connection beneath. This is a physiological fold formed by the force of opposing pressures: the palm and the joints of the fingers. The triangular area in the palm, known as the "Plain of Mars", is also caused, but in a more indirect way, by this pressure.

A great deal of experimental research has been done on the tactile *sensitivity* of the hand. Besides the topography of tactile sensitivity, we are now aware of the exact location of the tactile sensations, and even of the disorders of those sensations, in much greater detail than ever before. The skin not only perceives contact, but records it, analyzing its linear or other form. Two forms of tactile localisation have been distinguished: the *Ortsinn* of the Germans, the true location of tactile sensations, and the *Raumsinn,* or sense of place on the skin, in respect of which neurological research has produced some fascinating results.

This research, which has been refined and verified by modern methods, suggests that the palmar surface of the fingers, and in particular that of the finger-tips, ranks second on the scale of sensitivity. The first place is occupied by the tip of the tongue.

In this connection, one should remember

Vierordt's law: "The development of the sense of place of a particular part of the skin varies directly with the mobility of that part". The truth of this assertion has been verified for all parts of the body. Accordingly, one can appreciate the abundance and value of the information provided to us by the finger-tips.

As a result of his research, Gratiolet distinguished a new tactile sensation of the hand: "the sub-ungual touch". "However, the skin is sensitive throughout its whole thickness, and not merely at the surface. The skin may therefore receive impressions which may register on either of its two faces."

"The sensation of pressure begins when the sensitivity of the underlying surface comes into play. But a proper assessment of varying degrees of pressure requires new instruments. Here the nails play an important role. For example, when we apply the finger to the surface of some object, the slightest pressure moves the fleshy part, forcing it against the nail, as can be seen from the white areas which then form under the nail. This produces a curious sensation which moves from the front to the back of the finger-tip, and which can be designated "*sub-ungual touch*".

Men and women do not have the same tactile sensitivity; in the opinion of Lombroso, women are much less sensitive than men, in this respect. Galton and Randal, however, studied the relative sensitivity of the nape of the neck in men and women, and found women the more sensitive of the two sexes. According to W. Denett and A. Stern, there is no difference between the sexes, but there is a greater sensitivity found in well-educated people. Lombroso and Ottolenghi both found a distinct lack of sensitivity in the hands of criminals.

A writer spent a long time studying the case of a woman, named Marie Heurtin, who had been deaf, dumb and blind from birth, and wrote a highly interesting note on her subject's sense of smell and touch. "The thing one immediately notices is that her sense of smell and touch have attained a degree of refinement which is extremely rare in normal persons."

"Her sense of smell is so subtle that it usually enables her to recognize people, even before she has had a chance to touch them. Each individual seems to have, for her, a special smell, some distinctive quality, like the unmistakable, unique scent of a flower.

Speaking of the active sense of touch, he had this to say:

"The prodigious subtlety of this sense is particularly evident when Marie Heurtin tries to communicate with those around her. To form a clearer idea of what it must be like, just imagine that it is pitch dark and you must, for whatever reason, remain absolutely silent; and that, in these circumstances your hand happens to come in contact with the hand of a friend with whom you want to talk—all of a sudden, you will find that you have become capable of understanding the slightest movement of the hand, and of using such movements to express your innermost thoughts. Marie Heurtin is essentially in the same position, living in permanent darkness and total silence; for her, touch is the sole means of communication. Accordingly, as soon as her hand encounters another hand, it explores it, squeezes it and tries hard to detect the feelings of the other person. If she meets with no familiar response, only with inert fingers, her surprise and disappointment are immediately evident, and she withdraws her hand with visible regret. However, if the fingers come to life, her face promptly does likewise, and her fingers begin to talk. This mute language is incomparably impressive to behold. It is as if her very soul were

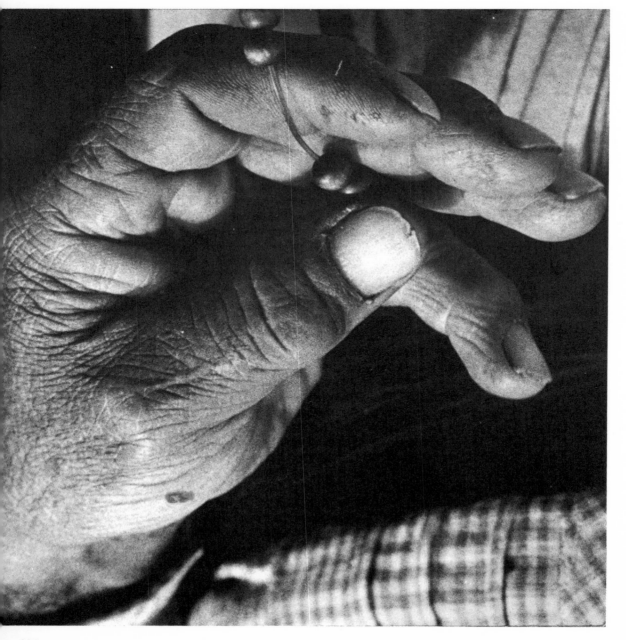

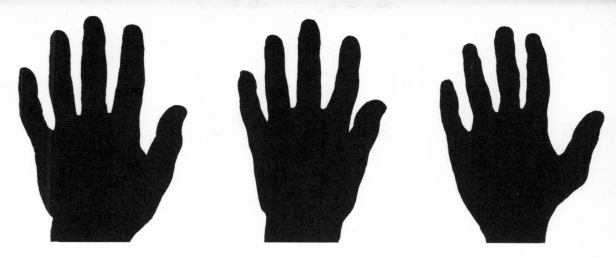

situated in her hand, and reaching out avidly to the world around her. She strains so intensely to perceive these tactile signals that she often understands a phrase which is only half-formulated, or may herself not even bother to complete the expression of her own thinking. If it were otherwise, of course, any conversation of appreciable length would quickly become extremely tedious. Once the pace of the conversation begins to quicken. Marie Heurtin, being blind, can perceive only fragmented movements and the bare outline of gestures; consequently, these fragments and outlines simply have to suffice. Sometimes, all she has to do is to touch Sister Margaret's wrist and feel the movements of her muscles in order to interpret her thinking, just as a musician might judge a melody, without actually hearing it, by the vibrations of the strings under his fingers.''

The chiromantist must know, at least empirically, that, in addition to the permanent anatomical protuberances, formed by the papillae of the dermis and their concentric curves, there are also temporary protuberances of the epidermis.

These are caused by a projection of the hair follicles, in the psycho-physiological process, whereby the skin takes on the appearance of "goose-flesh", particularly in cold weather, or after some violent emotional upheaval.

He must also be able to distinguish between the various creases and folds of the skin, and must not, for example, mistake the interpapillary creases with the muscular folds caused by fortuitous contractions of underlying muscle fibers, which may take widely differing forms. With the wear and tear of life, these folds eventually become imprinted on the skin in a permanent manner.

The chiromantist will also be able to distinguish between folds due to articulations and those due to movement.

He will also recognize that the most sensitive and mobile parts of the hand are situated on its outer edges, the palm being virtually immobile.

He will also study normal physiological distribution, and will empirically assess, from a qualitative point of view, the topographical layout of the hand.